THE BITTER CUP

WALKING WITH GOD WHEN YOUR WORLD FALLS APART

GUNTER AKRIDGE

HIGHER PERSPECTIVES
PRESS

Published by: Higher Perspectives Press

Edited by: Hope Myers

Design by: Shawn Barr

Paperback: ISBN 979-8-9926288-1-4
Hardcover: ISBN 979-8-9926288-2-1
Ebook: ISBN 979-8-9926288-3-8
Audiobook: ISBN 979-8-9926288-4-5

Dedication

To everyone who has walked through the fire and kept the faith. This is for you.

GUNTER AKRIDGE

Table of Contents

I have told you these things, so that in me you may have peace. In this world you will have trouble. But take heart! I have overcome the world.

John 16:33 NIV

INTRODUCTION

It's Not Supposed To Be This Way

I can still feel the shock and confusion I felt as a young boy, staring at my reflection in the bathroom mirror. It revealed a small, tear-streaked face with red cheeks and puffy eyes. The fluorescent lights above cast a harsh glare, making my countenance seem even more external and distant. Salty tears streamed down my face and onto my lips. My wails echoed off the bathroom walls, magnified by the hollow space.

My small hand gripped the edge of the sink, its cool porcelain surface providing some kind of anchor amid my emotions as I stared at my reflection. It was the first time I can remember seeing pain in my own eyes. I don't recall what horrible event could have caused such intense emotional turmoil, but the image of my tear-stained face remains etched in my mind. It was a raw and foreign feeling, a stinging grief that screamed of something being terribly wrong in my world.

At that moment, I realized that life was never meant to be filled with this kind of suffering. The pain in my eyes allowed me to see beyond myself, to understand the contrast between the broken state of the world and the way it should be. The way it was intended to be.

As I let go of some childlike innocence, I also let go of some of the ignorance in my young mind. Something inside me shifted, and I was suddenly faced with a harsh truth that I had never noticed before - the palpable reality of suffering, particularly my own. My heart, still young and naïve, protested as I stared back at my reflection in the bathroom mirror of my childhood home. Something in me insisted, "This isn't right. Life shouldn't be this way."

I can only imagine the weight that fell upon Adam and Eve when they became fully aware of their fallen state—and the broken world surrounding them. With one fateful bite, their world shattered into chaos. The couple now felt the sting of shame, suffering, and pain coursing through their veins. The death that had taken root within them would soon manifest physically as well. Their perfect existence was now tainted by sin and its consequences forever (Genesis 3).

It felt as though I had taken my own bite from the fruit of the tree of the knowledge of good and evil, and now I was staring into the depths of its effects on my soul. The weight of it seemed so much bigger than my own emotions could hold. My young mind was left wrestling with an ancient and universal truth: the existence of suffering.

No doubt you've also wrestled with the same hard truths about suffering in your own life.

"It's not supposed to be this way."

Maybe you've spoken similar words with tears streaming down your face, or maybe you've screamed them in the solitude of your own home or car where no one could hear. Suffering is a compulsory soundtrack always playing in the background of our story, although it may not be a melody we enjoy listening to.

I was six years old when I experienced the first major loss of a loved one. My paternal grandfather, Paw, the man I'd taken so many walks with down the dirt road, the man who had told me about Jesus while I sat in his lap (one of my earliest memories), the man who prayed over me and loved me immensely, suffered a major stroke and was suddenly gone from my life. I remember my dad coming to pick me up from school and breaking the news to me in the parking lot.

Days later, after the funeral, I drew a picture of the service, complete with my Paw in the casket at the front. It was my way of processing my grief and loss at that early age. I remember having to stuff the paper away because a member of the family had expressed visible emotional pain upon seeing it. I didn't want to make anyone more sad than they already were, so I hid my artwork and didn't speak of how I felt. It was my first lesson in hiding my own pain and grief.

Suffering didn't go away, even as I grew up. I learned to live with it, to accept it in some ways, to just keep going. Diagnosed with ADD (Attention Deficit Disorder), now known as ADHD (including "hyperactivity" into the acronym), school was extremely difficult for me. My pervading lens, which I experienced during my school career, was my own inability (or, you could even say, disability). "I'm so stupid," was my internal monologue nearly every day. It remains a persistent idea I keep having to squash even as an adult.

Miraculously, I overcame, graduating high school and going on to pursue a college degree and eventually, graduate studies. During my college years, I dealt with debilitating panic attacks and anxiety. Irrational fear and dread gripped my mind almost daily. Medication seemed to help enough to get me through, but my inability to cope with disappointment and other various stressors would continue into full adulthood. And honestly, anxiety and depression are still, to this day, all too frequent unwelcome visitors.

I didn't know it could get much worse. Within the first 2 years of marriage to my wife, Bethany, I was diagnosed with a blood cancer. Lymphoma. I underwent six months of chemotherapy, the hardest six months of my life at that point. The drugs that were being injected into me to rid me of the cancer cells that were coursing through my bloodstream simultaneously wreaked havoc on my body, my mind, and my emotions. As I began to lose my hair (all of it would be gone within weeks of treatment), my gag reflex would kick in as I pulled clumps of it from my head.

Cancer didn't just attack my body—it came for my mind, my emotions, and my sense of self. It's hard to explain how I felt during that season because, in many ways, I didn't feel the emotions as much as I leaked them. I remember standing in the shower, and suddenly, I was crying. No buildup. No obvious reason. Just a quiet overflow of grief that had been pooling somewhere deep inside me.

I grieved the strength I lost. I grieved the simple things I used to take for granted. That Christmas, I had to ask for help bringing our artificial tree into the house. It seems like such a small thing, but to me, it wasn't. It was another reminder that I wasn't who I used to be. Cancer had stripped away my ability to handle what I once did without a second thought. And if I wasn't strong, what did that make me? Less of a man? Less of me?

The anxiety was relentless. The "what ifs" took up space in my mind day and night. What if the treatments weren't working? What if this was all for nothing? What if I died? That thought stayed with me, hovering just over my shoulder, whispering in moments when I was too exhausted to resist it.

At one point, I wrestled with whether I even wanted to keep going. The treatments were brutal, and I wasn't sure I could endure a few more rounds of something that might not even save me. I almost didn't finish. I was ready to quit. But Bethany—steady, strong, and seeing beyond my exhaustion—pushed me forward. She had to talk me into those last few treatments. I didn't want to go, but she made sure I did

Depression settled in like an unwelcome guest. It didn't always look like sadness—it often looked like nothing. Just emptiness. A numbness that made everything feel distant, like I was watching my life happen rather than living it. I had moments where I laughed, where I had good days, but there was always something underneath. The weight of it all never really left.

Even after treatment ended, the struggle didn't. I expected relief, but what I got was another battle—one that didn't leave physical scars but left plenty of others. It was the battle of figuring out how to live again when cancer had rewritten so much of who I was. And beneath it all, I carried a quiet, lingering guilt—why did I get to survive when so many others didn't? Cancer is an awful, awful experience. But I made it through and was declared "in remission" from the disease that tried to claim my life at twenty-four years old.

The fear of my cancer coming back is always there, even when I don't talk about it. It shows up in doctor visits, random pains, or just thinking about the future. Being a survivor isn't just about getting past it—it's carrying the scars, the side effects, and the way life is forever split into "before" and "after." It's learning to live with both gratitude and uncertainty, trusting God with each day, even when the fear tries to creep in.

Today, as a parent, I've experienced the inexpressible joy of watching my kids grow up and become amazing human beings. But I've also felt the gut-wrenching pain and grief of watching them walk their own path of suffering, seemingly unable to save them from it. Sometimes, all I can do is guide and protect, but ultimately become a spectator to their own struggles with pain, anxiety, and grief.

My point in telling my stories is this: I'm human. And I'm writing this book from the perspective of someone who has walked through devastating seasons of pain and suffering just like you, the reader, have.

As a pastor for many years, I've prayed with many people who suffer from chronic pain and illness. I've stood at the bedside of many patients who are scared and just need someone to be there during their sickness. I've sat with families who have just received devastating news concerning their child. I've embraced those still reeling from the sudden loss of a spouse or parent. None of us are strangers to suffering. It has visited us all.

As I write this book, the Middle Eastern conflict rages on with no end in sight. The airwaves are flooded with 24/7 news coverage, bombarding us with disturbing images that are almost too painful to watch. Meanwhile, there are the looming threats of World War III from dictatorial governments, their leaders' voices echoing across the airwaves and seeping into our psyche, further heightening the collective anxiety that grips our planet.

It is a time of great turmoil and uncertainty, where every day brings a new wave of unsettling news and events. The current state of the world is filled with suffering and turmoil, not only in faraway lands but also close to our own homes and lives. It is a weight we must all grapple with, no matter how much we may try to push it away.

Suffering is a human experience, as much as we hate it. But so is joy. My hopes are to help you, reader and fellow sufferer, to build a bridge between those two seemingly diametrically opposed themes—joy and suffering. Because it is possible to find joy in suffering, as ridiculous or even offensive as that sounds. Furthermore, it is possible–I would even say highly likely– to find God Himself in the middle of suffering.

I will take it a step further and say that it is necessary to do so. Finding Him in our hardest moments offers us something better than the elusive answers to the myriad of questions suffering thrusts upon us. Answers we think we need to move on with life, to find meaning and purpose in it. But the truth is, we might not have all the answers. We probably won't get most of our hardest questions answered as much as we ask, seek, study, pray, and even beg.

Mystery is just that—mystery. But the hope I want to dangle before your possibly broken and exhausted heart is that God can be found in the middle of the mystery, and yes, even the suffering and devastation that comes into our lives. As we move forward, we'll wrestle with some of life's hardest questions. Why does suffering exist? Is there any meaning behind it, or is it all random? What does God have to say about our pain, and can He really be found in the middle of it? Along the way, we'll confront some common myths about suffering—ideas that can weigh us down rather than lift us up—and search for a deeper understanding of how faith intersects with pain.

This book isn't just a theological or philosophical exercise. It's deeply personal. It's written by someone who has faced the kind of heartbreak that makes you cry out, "This isn't fair." I don't have all the answers, but I believe there is a God who walks with us through the fire, a God who doesn't shy away from our hardest questions or deepest grief.

We'll take a close look at the life of Jesus, the man of sorrows, and ask what it means to follow a Savior who walked through suffering Himself. We'll also explore how community plays a vital role in helping us bear the weight of grief. Let the stories included in the following pages of people who have endured offer you strength and hope. Ultimately, this is a journey toward finding joy and hope—not in spite of suffering, but within it.

You don't have to have all the answers to walk this path. In fact, you might leave with more questions than when you started. But I hope by the time we reach the end, you'll feel more equipped to face suffering with honesty, courage, and a renewed sense of God's presence.

So, let's journey together. Let's wrestle with the hard questions, embrace the mystery, and search for the joy and hope that can only be found in the midst of the struggle. There's no neat, tidy bow to wrap around suffering, but there is a God who promises to meet us in it.

CHAPTER ONE

SOLVING THE PUZZLE OF PAIN

The word suffering has become so broad that it's almost lost its meaning. It's a word that tries to capture a vast range of experiences, from heartbreak to illness to injustice, and it means something different to everyone. Our understanding of suffering is shaped by our own pain or by the stories of others who've shared their struggles with us. But defining suffering is important—it helps us "put a face to a name," so to speak. This isn't just about a concept or an idea. Suffering is a tangible, unavoidable reality in our lives. And if we're going to address it, we need to be clear about what it truly is.

"No statement, theological or otherwise, should be made that would not be credible in the presence of burning children."

This harrowing statement is from Holocaust scholar

Irving Greenberg. His words were shaped by the atrocities of the Holocaust, where millions, including children, were brutally murdered. It's a stark reminder that before we try to explain suffering, we must face its harsh and painful reality, avoiding shallow or abstract answers that don't respect the depth of human pain.

Elie Wiesel's memoir *Night* offers a profound and distressing account of his spiritual struggle during the Holocaust. As a devout Jewish teenager from Sighet, Romania, Elie began his journey with an unshakable faith in God. However, his experiences in Auschwitz and other concentration camps led him to wrestle deeply with his beliefs.

One of these disturbing experiences was the public hanging of a young boy who was loved by many in the camp. The boy was accused of sabotage and, as punishment, was hanged alongside two men. Unlike the men, the boy was too light to die instantly, and he hung struggling for over half an hour as the prisoners were forced to watch. Someone behind Elie whispered, "Where is God now?"

Elie, tormented by the scene, reflected that God seemed absent. He writes: *"Where is He? Here He is—He is hanging here on this gallows."*

This moment shattered Elie's faith, marking the beginning of a profound spiritual crisis. From that point on, his relationship with God was no longer one of devotion but of doubt, anger, and silence as he struggled to reconcile his suffering with the idea of a just and merciful deity. He questioned how a good and omnipotent God could allow such suffering and cruelty, especially to innocent children.

While Wiesel survived the Holocaust, his faith was

never the same. Yet, his life became a testament to the importance of memory, compassion, and the struggle to find meaning in a world marred by evil. His story captures not only the horrors of the Holocaust but also the profound spiritual and existential questions that arose in its wake. When we think about the other various atrocities recorded in our history books, the sheer scale of suffering is almost too much to comprehend. It's truly overwhelming.

And we ask ourselves, why? Why all this pain? Is there any purpose in suffering, or is it all just senseless? What can possibly soothe our souls when we stand face-to-face with its raw, unyielding weight?

Thinking Through Pain

Since the beginning of human history, questions have been asked and wrestled with in the face of such suffering—questions of "why" and "where is God in all of this" echo throughout history.

When faced with suffering, the question of meaning often consumes our thoughts. We naturally ask why such horrific tragedies occur. Is there a purpose behind the pain? Or is it all simply random chance? The greatest philosophers and religious leaders have explored these questions for ages. The problem of suffering is not new.

I know it's probably a bit early to plunge headfirst into the deep waters of philosophy and theology to tackle humanity's oldest existential question. But hey, why not? After all, the question "why is there suffering?" has been humanity's constant companion since the beginning. And while we might not come away with a perfectly satisfactory answer (spoiler: we won't), exploring how others have wrestled with it can give us perspective and maybe even a little comfort.

From ancient philosophers scribbling in scrolls to modern-day thinkers typing furiously on their laptops, countless people have grappled with the same questions you and I face today. Why does pain exist? Does it serve a purpose, or is it just random chaos? These aren't just abstract, ivory-tower debates—they're deeply human questions. They're the questions we ask late at night when life feels overwhelming, when loss hits too close to home, or when we're simply trying to make sense of things when our world falls apart.

Understanding how others have approached this question throughout history helps us in two ways. First, it reassures us that we're not alone. You're not the only one asking, "Why?" People from every culture, religion, and era have been asking it too. Second, it gives us a kind of roadmap—not necessarily answers, but perspectives that can guide us as we navigate our own struggles. Think of it like borrowing someone else's flashlight to help you see just a little more clearly.

We're not just here to look at how suffering has been explained. We're here to gain insight into how it's been endured—and even transformed—by those who came before us. Let's take a closer look at how humans, from ancient thinkers to modern minds, have wrestled with this question and what we can learn from them.

When Life Hands You Lemons...

You've probably heard the old adage, "When life hands you lemons, make lemonade." Believe it or not, that's philosophy! It's giving us all a way to look at hardship pragmatically, to take the bad and make the best of it. I'll utilize these lemons to illustrate how each philosophical school would apply it.

The Ancient Greeks

Some of the earliest philosophical explorations we have available to us are those of the ancient Greek thinkers:

Stoicism: Stoicism emerged in the 4th century BCE through Zeno of Citium and was later developed by philosophers like Epictetus and Marcus Aurelius. The Stoics taught that suffering was an inevitable part of life but could be managed by focusing on internal responses rather than external circumstances. Virtue, they argued, is the only true good, and it is within our control, unlike wealth, health, or reputation. In his Meditations, Marcus Aurelius emphasizes acceptance of suffering as part of nature's order, encouraging rational detachment from pain.

Simply put, the Stoics would probably replace the old "when life hands you lemons" adage with something more like…"Forget lemonade—just accept the lemons and stay chill about it."

Plato: In his *Republic* and other dialogues, Plato viewed suffering as a result of living in the imperfect material world. According to Plato, true reality exists in the realm of Forms—perfect, unchanging ideals that our physical world only imitates. Therefore, suffering reflects the inherent flaws of the material world and can only be transcended by seeking the higher knowledge of these Forms.

Plato would say, "Those aren't real lemons—true lemons exist in the perfect, unchanging realm of Forms. Aim higher, folks!"

Aristotle: Aristotle offered a more practical approach, viewing suffering as an opportunity for cultivating virtue. He argued that suffering, when met with courage and wisdom, contributes to achieving true happiness, the ultimate goal of human life. For Aristotle, suffering is not intrinsically good, but it can serve as a stepping stone to moral excellence.

"When life hands you lemons," Aristotle would have said, "Use them to build character—and maybe a profitable lemonade stand while you're at it."

Eastern Philosophy

Buddhism: Founded by Siddhartha Gautama (the Buddha) in the 5th–4th century BCE, Buddhism explains that suffering (dukkha) is at the heart of life. The Buddha proposed the *Four Noble Truths* and the *Eightfold Path* as a way to overcome it and achieve enlightenment—nirvana. And no, it's not just a grunge band; it's the ultimate freedom from all the world's angst.

"When life hands you lemons," according to the Buddha, "It's your craving for lemonade that's the real problem—let go of that, and you'll find peace."

Taoism and Confucianism: Taoism, taught by Laozi in the *Tao Te Ching*, focuses on living in harmony with the Tao, the natural flow of the universe. Struggling against this flow, often due to desires and ambitions, leads to suffering. The key is to embrace simplicity and humility, to go with the flow.

Confucianism, founded in the 6th century BCE, sees suffering as the result of broken relationships and chaos. By practicing respect and integrity and fulfilling your duties, harmony can be restored, reducing suffering in society.

"When life hands you lemons," Laozi would say, "Go with the flow and make nature-friendly lemonade," while Confucius would add, "And don't forget to share it with your neighbors."

Hinduism: Hinduism, one of the world's oldest religions, teaches that suffering is part of *samsara*, the endless cycle of birth, death, and rebirth. Our actions, or karma, decide the struggles we face in this life or the next. The ultimate goal, moksha (liberation), is to escape the cycle by living rightly, practicing spirituality, and seeking self-discovery. It's about owning your actions while striving for enlightenment.

"When life hands you lemons," Hinduism says, "Maybe you planted the lemon tree in a past life."

Medieval Philosophies

Christian Philosophy: St. Augustine believed suffering was a result of human sin but also saw it as a way for God to refine believers and shift their focus from temporary pleasures to eternal salvation. In *City of God*, he explained how suffering fits into God's larger plan for redemption. Later, Thomas Aquinas expanded on Augustine's ideas by combining Aristotle's philosophy with Christian theology in *Summa Theologica*. Aquinas viewed suffering as part of divine justice, with the promise of ultimate restoration in the afterlife.

"When life hands you lemons," these Church fathers would say, "Those sour moments teach you to crave heaven's sweetness," or respectively, "Some things are better than lemonade!"

Islamic Philosophy: Al-Ghazali and Averroes, two prominent Islamic thinkers, tackled suffering from different angles. Al-Ghazali saw it as a test of faith and a chance for spiritual growth, encouraging patience and trust in God. Averroes focused on understanding suffering through rational thought, aiming to balance faith with philosophical reasoning.

"When life hands you lemons," Al-Ghazali would encourage, "It's a test—stay faithful," while Averroes would reply, "Let's analyze these lemons rationally before we juice them."

The Enlightenment and Rationalism

David Hume and Voltaire: In *Dialogues Concerning Natural Religion*, Hume argued that unnecessary suffering challenges the idea of an all-good, all-powerful God. This "problem of evil" remains a major philosophical issue. Similarly, Voltaire's *Candide* used humor to mock the idea that suffering always serves a higher purpose. Instead, Voltaire emphasized taking action to address suffering rather than relying on blind optimism.

Philosophers like Hume and Voltaire would ask, 'Why would a good God allow lemons in the first place?"

Modern and Postmodern Perspectives

Nietzsche and Existentialism: Friedrich Nietzsche believed suffering didn't need a divine explanation. Instead, he saw it as a chance for growth if faced with courage. Later, Jean-Paul Sartre argued that life has no meaning unless we create it, and we must confront suffering ourselves. Both rejected religion as an answer, focusing on personal responsibility.

Contemporary Philosophy: Modern thinkers like Martha Nussbaum focus on practical ways to address suffering. She emphasizes using empathy, compassion, and ethical actions to understand and ease others' pain.

Nietzsche would counter, "Crush those lemons with your very will!" (*in a German accent, of course) Meanwhile, Nussbaum would quietly suggest, "Maybe just listen to someone else who's struggling with their own lemons."

Judaic Perspective

Judaism: Rooted in the *Tanakh* (Jewish Scriptures), Judaism doesn't offer a single answer to suffering but provides ways to engage with it. This includes embracing its mystery, lamenting, trusting in God's justice, and taking action to repair the world. Rabbinical writings like the *Mishnah*, *Talmud*, and *Midrashim* build on the *Tanakh*, reflecting on the purpose, meaning, and response to suffering.

Christianity

I've saved the Christian worldview on suffering for the end of this section—not because it's going to give us the most definitive answers, but because it's the centerpiece of this book. Let me be honest: the doctrines of the Christian faith don't always wrap up the problem of suffering in a way that fully satisfies the intellect or completely soothes a wounded soul.

But what Christianity does offer—uniquely—is context. It invites us into a relationship with a God who can be known, a God who doesn't always give us the answers we're looking for or deliver us from suffering the way we'd hope, but a God who chooses to walk with us through it.

We'll spend plenty of time unpacking this in the chapters ahead, but for now, I want to lay the groundwork. Let's explore the views on suffering held by different parts of the Church over the centuries. The goal is to gain a fuller, more nuanced understanding of how Christians have grappled with this mystery so we're better equipped to move forward.

The Theodicies

When faced with the reality of suffering, theologians, philosophers, and believers have developed various frameworks, called *theodicies*, to reconcile the existence of a good and powerful God with the pain and evil in the world. These theodicies do not provide definitive answers, but they offer perspectives that can help us grapple with the mystery of suffering. Here's a closer look at some of the most explored theodicies that have sought to answer the question, "If God exists and is good, why is there suffering in the world?"

Suffering As A Result of Free Will

The first theodicy we'll examine is The Free Will Theodicy. This view emphasizes that God created humans with the ability to make free choices, a necessary condition for genuine love and moral responsibility. However, this freedom also allows for the possibility of sin and evil. According to this view, much of the suffering in the world arises from the misuse of free will—both by individuals and by humanity collectively. This would encompass moral evil and natural evil.

Moral evil includes human actions such as violence, greed, and cruelty. People suffer because of the poor moral choices of others. That's just a fact. And we all have experienced that first hand. But what about suffering that has little or nothing to do with human will or action? What about natural disasters, diseases, and the like? Well, some would argue (especially those using the Bible to explain this) that natural disasters and similar tragedies are simply a result of "the Fall" of man, which disrupted and corrupted nature itself (Genesis 3).

Augustine, one of the early proponents of this theodicy, argued that evil results from humanity's turning away from God, not from any flaw in God's creation. So, according to Augustine, none of the blame is on God; it's on all of us. But one might ask why God seems to not be actively trying to stop it. Does God even have to try? Can't he just eradicate suffering and be done with it?

Some have declared that God does not interfere with free will because doing so would negate its purpose and render humanity's love for Him meaningless. After all, love requires choice, and without free will, true love cannot exist. This perspective emphasizes human accountability and offers some explanation for the existence of moral evil in a way that seems to preserve God's goodness.

But does it really? After all, God is still allowing it to happen, isn't He? He might not be orchestrating the hurricane (though some would argue He is), but He's also not stopping it. So, while the free will argument sheds light on certain aspects of suffering, it still falls short of fully answering the question.

Suffering As A Means of Growth

According to this perspective, the challenges, hardships, and adversities we face are not arbitrary or accidental but woven into the fabric of existence to help us become more virtuous. Without suffering, humanity would remain spiritually immature, incapable of developing traits like courage, patience, and compassion.

This view contrasts sharply with the idea of a perfect, pain-free paradise. Instead of creating a world where humans exist in a state of moral perfection from the outset, God designed a world where individuals must struggle, make choices, and grow through their experiences. This process transforms the soul, preparing it for a deeper relationship with God.

John Hick, a prominent 20th-century philosopher and theologian, is credited with the "Soul-Making Theodicy," the official name of this view. He described the world as a "vale of soul-making"—a place purposefully designed by God to challenge humanity and foster spiritual growth. He explained,

> *"God has created us as immature creatures in order to put us through the process of soul-making, that is, of creating saints and children of God."*

It's true that suffering can refine character, deepen empathy, and draw us closer to God. It's not meaningless—it serves a transformative purpose. And that should give us hope in our struggles. Biblical themes align closely with this idea. The Apostle Paul writes in Romans 5:3–4 that suffering produces perseverance, character, and hope. James 1:2–4 similarly encourages believers to consider trials as opportunities for growth, noting that the testing of faith produces endurance and maturity. Even Irenaeus, an early church father, believed humanity was created immature and must grow into the likeness of God through life's trials.

Even so, this can feel insufficient in the face of extreme or senseless suffering, such as the death of a child or a terminal illness. And furthermore, it certainly raises questions about why a loving God couldn't create a world where growth occurs without pain. I don't know about you, but "becoming a better person" isn't good enough for me when I'm grieving a massive loss. It falls short of a satisfactory answer.

Suffering And The Greater Good

This particular theodicy suggests that God allows suffering because it contributes to a greater good that might not be immediately apparent. Some events that seem senseless or cruel may have long-term purposes that only God can see. This perspective often relies on the belief that God can bring beauty and redemption out of brokenness.

It's true that God's ultimate plan includes the redemption of all things (Revelation 21:4), and temporary suffering is part of a larger story that culminates in eternal joy. That's really good news! This certainly provides hope by focusing on God's power to bring good out of evil. It's a lot easier to view our suffering through the lens of God's overall plan of making all things right and good.

The Bible supports the idea that God uses suffering to achieve good, even if the reasons remain hidden at the time. Take the story of Joseph, for example. He was sold into slavery by his brothers and, later imprisoned, declares, "You intended to harm me, but God intended it for good to accomplish what is now being done, the saving of many lives" (Genesis 50:20). His suffering led to the salvation of Egypt and his family during a famine.

Paul describes suffering as temporary and transformative: "For our light and momentary troubles are achieving for us an eternal glory that far outweighs them all" (2 Corinthians 4:17). There's no question that God can turn things around for our good and His glory. But what about the present? When you're in pain, the vague promise of a better future doesn't always bring comfort to the here and now.

This can feel really dismissive when applied too casually. I once stood in line at a funeral and overheard someone tell a grieving mother mourning the loss of her young son, *"Everything happens for a reason."* Statements like this, though often well-intentioned, can diminish the raw and immediate pain of loss, making it seem as though suffering is insignificant or easily explained away.

But the question remains. Why can't a loving and omnipotent God achieve these greater goods without allowing so much suffering? Couldn't an all-powerful God create a world where growth and redemption occur without pain? This viewpoint struggles to fully account for instances of extreme suffering, such as genocide or the abuse of children, where the "greater good" may not be discernible, even in hindsight.

Suffering And Cosmic Conflict

The Warfare Worldview explains suffering as the result of a cosmic struggle between God and the forces of evil, particularly Satan and his demonic forces. Unlike perspectives that frame suffering as a tool in God's hands or as a natural consequence of human free will, this view emphasizes the active opposition of spiritual beings to God's purposes. It portrays suffering as collateral damage in a broader battle, one in which God is not the author of evil but the ultimate victor over it.

This perspective identifies Satan and his forces as the primary instigators of much of the world's pain and suffering. The Bible portrays Satan as an adversary whose goal is to steal, kill, and destroy (John 10:10). His influence is seen in natural disasters, illnesses, temptations, and moral evil. For example, in the Book of Job, Satan is directly responsible for Job's suffering, inflicting loss, disease, and devastation with God's permission (Job 1:6–12; Job 2:1–7).

Central to the Warfare Worldview is the life and ministry of Jesus, which is depicted as a direct confrontation with the powers of darkness. Jesus healed the sick, cast out demons, and preached the coming of God's kingdom—a kingdom that would ultimately overthrow Satan's rule. His death and resurrection are seen as the decisive victory in this cosmic conflict (Colossians 2:15).

So, Jesus' exorcisms are not merely acts of healing but incremental victories over Satan's dominion (Matthew 12:28). While Christ has won the ultimate victory, the Warfare Worldview emphasizes that believers are still engaged in the ongoing battle against evil. Paul writes in Ephesians 6:12 that the struggle is not against "flesh and blood" but against "spiritual forces of evil in the heavenly realms." Christians are called to take up the "armor of God" (Ephesians 6:13–18), engaging in spiritual practices like prayer, fasting, and faith to resist the enemy's schemes.

This perspective reassures believers that God is not the author of evil but is actively working against it. It presents God as a compassionate ally who fights alongside humanity rather than a distant figure, allowing suffering for mysterious purposes. This idea that God cares and is fighting for us in our battles inspires hope. It not only reminds us that we will win one day, ultimately. But it also gives us something to do about it. We can actively "wage war" against the forces that are causing the destruction.

Personally, I have gravitated toward this theodicy in recent years. It seems odd that the knowledge of being engaged in a spiritual battle actually encourages me to stay in it. I mean, after all, it's better to believe that God is fighting for me rather than fighting against me, merely watching me suffer or, worse, potentially causing it for some "greater good."

However, this view does have notable limitations. One common critique is its tendency to attribute every instance of suffering, illness, or hardship to demonic activity—the old "devil behind every bush" way of looking at the world. This overemphasis can overshadow other contributing factors, such as human responsibility, natural laws, or the consequences of living in a fallen world.

While the Warfare Worldview highlights God's opposition to suffering, it doesn't fully address a key question: why does an all-powerful God allow the forces of evil to exist and act? And, perhaps even more unsettling, it raises the question—what if God isn't truly stronger than these evil forces and is locked in an ongoing struggle? That possibility is anything but reassuring. These theological challenges demand careful consideration, as they leave some crucial questions unanswered.

Quite frankly, none of the arguments presented above thus far are good enough for a parent who is sitting by the bedside of their dying child. And let's be honest, they don't suffice for us either when we're facing our own little Hell on earth.

Suffering And Mystery

The Appeal to Mystery theodicy takes a different approach to suffering. Instead of trying to explain or solve it, this perspective invites us to acknowledge that some things are simply beyond human understanding. It's the idea that God's ways are higher than ours (Isaiah 55:8–9) and that His reasons for allowing suffering are often hidden from us. But rather than giving us all the answers, God offers something even better: His presence.

This view clearly shows up in Job's story. Job loses everything—his family, health, livelihood—and he's desperate for an explanation. He cries out to God, asking why.

But when God finally speaks, He doesn't give Job the reasons behind his suffering. Instead, He points to His own power and wisdom, asking Job questions like, "Where were you when I laid the earth's foundation?" (Job 38:4). It's not the answer Job was looking for, but it's enough to remind him that God is in control, even when life feels out of control. Job's response is humble: "Surely I spoke of things I did not understand, things too wonderful for me to know" (Job 42:3).

The Appeal to Mystery reminds us that faith doesn't require us to have all the answers. Instead, it invites us to trust God's character—His goodness, wisdom, and justice—even when life doesn't make sense.

This idea is echoed by Samuel Terrien in his book *The Elusive Presence*. Terrien writes of how God's presence often feels hidden or distant, especially in times of suffering. But that doesn't mean He's absent. God may not always explain why we're going through pain, but He promises to be with us in it. That presence, even when it feels elusive, is what sustains us.

Walter Brueggemann adds another layer to this in

his writings on the Psalms. He points out that the Psalms give us permission to be honest with God about our pain. They're full of raw questions like, *"How long, O Lord?" and "Why have you forsaken me?"* Brueggemann calls this "lament" and says it's not a sign of weak faith but deep trust. When we cry out to God, we're not giving up on Him— we're reaching for Him, even when we don't understand.

The Appeal to Mystery offers a lot of hope if you're willing to embrace it. It doesn't try to sugarcoat suffering or tie it up in a neat little bow. Instead, it says, "You don't have to understand everything. Just trust the One who does." That shift can take the pressure off, especially when we're in the middle of something we can't explain.

Embracing mystery in this way helps us focus on relationship instead of resolution. Instead of trying to figure out all the reasons behind our suffering, we can focus on experiencing God's presence in it. Faith isn't about solving the mystery; it's about trusting that God is with us in the middle of it.

But let's be honest—this perspective isn't always easy to accept. If you like concrete answers, the Appeal to Mystery can feel frustrating or dismissive. When you're hurting, it's hard to hear, *"Just trust God."* It can feel like a cop-out, even if it's true.

There's also the risk of using this approach in the wrong way. Saying, *"God's ways are higher than ours,"* can come across as dismissive if it's not paired with real empathy. People need to feel seen and heard in their pain, not brushed off with a quick theological statement. Jesus, help us guard our lips!

Mystery doesn't give us all the answers, and that's the point. It invites us to let go of the need to understand everything and to trust in God's goodness, even when life feels unfair or confusing. This isn't about blind faith—it's about honest faith. It's about crying out to God when we're hurting and trusting that He hears us, even when His plans don't make sense to us.

So, while this perspective may not satisfy every question, it gives us a framework to hold onto God in the middle of the unknown. And sometimes, that's enough.

The Hardest Question

In Matthew 20:20–28, we find an interaction that's both bold and a little cringeworthy. James and John, the sons of Zebedee, don't just approach Jesus with a request—they bring their mom along for backup. She steps forward and says, "Grant that one of these two sons of mine may sit at your right and the other at your left in your kingdom." You can almost feel the tension as the other disciples look on, probably muttering, "Seriously? Did they just ask that?"

It's easy to roll our eyes at the audacity of the request. But honestly, don't we all kind of do the same thing? We crave the spotlight, recognition, and reward without fully understanding what it takes to get there. We want the glory, but we don't want the grind. James and John's question isn't just their misunderstanding; it's ours, too.

Jesus' response cuts through their ambition and strikes at the heart of discipleship. He doesn't say, "No way," or laugh them off. Instead, He asks, "Can you drink the cup I am going to drink?" The "cup" He's talking about isn't a trophy or a toast—it's the cup of suffering. It's the betrayal, the beatings, the humiliation, the cross. It's the bitter cost of redemption.

In their confidence—or ignorance—James and John reply, "We can." And Jesus doesn't contradict them. Instead, He says, "You will indeed drink from my cup, but to sit at my right or left is not for me to grant. These places belong to those for whom they have been prepared by my Father." They didn't know it yet, but their paths would lead them down roads of suffering and sacrifice. James would be the first of the apostles to be martyred (Acts 12:2), and John would endure exile on the island of Patmos (Revelation 1:9). The cup wasn't just for Jesus—it was for them, too.

This moment is such a snapshot of human nature. James and John thought they were asking for status, power, and VIP seats in Jesus' kingdom. But they didn't understand what they were really signing up for. Jesus' kingdom doesn't operate like the kingdoms of this world. It's not about climbing the ladder or securing a title. It's about humility. Service. Suffering. The very things we naturally want to avoid.

Jesus doesn't crush their ambition; He just redirects it. "Whoever wants to become great among you must be your servant, and whoever wants to be first must be your slave— just as the Son of Man did not come to be served, but to serve, and to give his life as a ransom for many" (Matthew 20:26–28).

It's such a reversal of how we think greatness works. In

Jesus' kingdom, the way up is down. The path to glory runs straight through the valley of suffering. And that's hard to swallow.

This isn't the only time Jesus talks about the cup. In the Garden of Gethsemane, just hours before His arrest, He falls on His face and prays, "My Father, if it is possible, may this cup be taken from me. Yet not as I will, but as you will" (Matthew 26:39). The weight of it is overwhelming. Even Jesus, in His humanity, pleads for another way. But He still drinks the cup, fully and willingly.

And that's what makes this image so powerful. The cup isn't just a symbol of suffering; it's a symbol of obedience. Jesus drank the cup not because it was easy but because it was necessary. Through His suffering, redemption was poured out for us.

Here's the thing about Jesus' question to James and John: it's not just for them. It's for us, too. "Can you drink the cup I am going to drink?" It's a hard question because we know what the cup represents. It's the suffering we don't want to face, the sacrifices we don't want to make, the obedience that costs more than we'd like to give. The bitter cup is often discarded and unwanted.

No one in their right mind would say yes to this question…unless they knew that there was something of immeasurable value to be had by drinking of it. Something so unbelievably good that even the horrors of suffering can't hold a candle to it.

And yet, Jesus doesn't call us to drink the cup alone. The same Savior who walked the path of suffering walks it with us. The same God who drank the bitter cup transforms our suffering into something redemptive. The cup we're called to drink may be hard, but it's not hopeless. It's part of a story where suffering is not the end but a means to glory.

As you read this, maybe you're already holding your own "cup." Maybe it's the pain of loss, the weight of illness, or the exhaustion of trying to be faithful in a world that doesn't make it easy. Whatever it is, know this: Jesus drank the cup first. He knows the bitterness. He knows the cost. And He knows the glory that comes after.

The story about James and John isn't just a lesson in humility; it's an invitation. Jesus invites you to trust Him with your cup. To let Him walk with you through it. To believe that, even in the suffering, there's a purpose. Because in His kingdom, the cup isn't the end of the story—it's the beginning of something eternal.

CHAPTER TWO

BORN FOR TROUBLE

Yet man is born to trouble as surely as sparks fly upward.
Job 5:7 NIV

Suffering is the universal thread woven through every human life. No matter our background, beliefs, or choices, trouble finds us all. It's as inevitable as gravity, as unrelenting as time. But what makes suffering so fascinating—and frustrating—is that it doesn't affect us all the same way.

Some people emerge from pain with their faith intact, even strengthened. Others find themselves disillusioned, walking away from God entirely. What makes the difference? Is it the intensity of the suffering? The timing? Or is it something deeper—something about how we understand God and suffering itself?

To explore this, let's look at two contrasting stories: one of faith that stands firm and one that crumbles under the weight of pain.

Faith Shipwrecked

Take Sarah, for example. She grew up in a church-going family, memorizing Bible verses and singing hymns every Sunday. Her faith was strong—or so it seemed. She had built her life around believing that God would protect and bless her if she followed Him. And for a while, that belief held true. Sarah married her college sweetheart, Ryan, and together they built a beautiful life—two healthy kids, a cozy home, and plans for a future filled with laughter and love.

But one ordinary Tuesday morning, everything changed. As Sarah was making breakfast for her children, the phone rang. It was the hospital. Ryan had been in a car accident. A distracted driver had run a red light at full speed, slamming into Ryan's car. The doctors did everything they could, but the injuries were too severe. Just like that, the love of Sarah's life was gone.

At first, Sarah clung to her faith, desperate for peace, answers, or some sense of God's presence. But as days turned into weeks and then months, all she felt was silence. Friends from church dropped by with casseroles and Bible verses, but their words often stung more than they soothed. "Everything happens for a reason," one well-meaning friend told her, but Sarah couldn't reconcile those words with the deep void of Ryan's absence.

As time went on, Sarah found it harder and harder to pray. The God she had trusted to protect her family now felt distant, even cruel. She stopped going to church, unable to sit in a pew surrounded by happy families, reminded of what she'd lost. Slowly, the faith that had once been the foundation of her life began to crumble.

Sarah didn't wake up one day and decide to leave her faith behind. It was a slow drift, like a boat untied from the dock. Her pain, her questions, and her anger felt too big to bring to God, and over time, she stopped trying.

Faith Sustained

Now consider James. He also faced unimaginable pain—the loss of his teenage daughter, Emma, to a rare illness. James and his wife, Megan, had prayed relentlessly for a miracle. They rallied their church and community, clinging to the belief that God could heal their daughter. Every night, James knelt beside Emma's hospital bed, begging God for her life.

But the miracle never came. After months of grueling treatments, Emma's body gave out. James held her hand as she slipped away, the sound of her labored breathing replaced by a silence that felt unbearable.

James was devastated. In the days that followed, he spent a lot of time in a nearby chapel, staring at the stained-glass window of Jesus on the cross. He didn't know what to pray. "Why?" he whispered into the empty room. "Why her? Why not me?"

His grief was raw, his questions unrelenting. But James didn't let go of God. Instead, he brought his pain to Him, pouring out his anger, his doubts, and his heartbreak. It wasn't pretty and didn't feel holy, but it was honest.

At Emma's funeral, James stood before the congregation and shared through tears, "I don't understand why this happened. I don't have the answers. But I know this: God was with Emma in her suffering, and He's with us now. He hasn't abandoned us, even when it feels like the darkness swallows us whole."

James's faith wasn't unshaken—it had been battered and bruised—but it held. Through his pain, he found that God's presence was enough, even when His answers were not.

What Makes The Difference?

What makes Sarah's and James's stories so compelling isn't the difference in their suffering—it's the difference in their response. Sarah's faith was built on believing that God's goodness meant her life would be free from tragedy. When that belief was challenged, her faith lacked the depth to withstand the storm.

James, on the other hand, had a faith that made room for grief and questions. His theology didn't promise him a life free from pain, but it gave him hope that God could be trusted, even in the midst of it. That trust didn't erase his suffering, but it sustained him through it.

These stories reveal a powerful truth: suffering exposes the foundation of our faith. Everyone has a theology of suffering—whether well-formed or fragile. And suffering tests and reveals the strength of that theology. Is it rooted in a shallow understanding of God, or in a deep trust in His character? Sarah and James faced the same question: "Can I trust God in my suffering?" Their answers shaped the trajectory of their lives.

Taking Off The Mask

The Church desperately needs a stronger, more honest theology of suffering—one that isn't flimsy or fragile but built to endure the storms of life. Too often, modern Christianity has been reduced to a message of perpetual happiness, where walking with God is equated with having a life free of trouble. We've traded the hard truths of faith for slogans like, *"I'm too blessed to be stressed, brother!"* And while that may sound nice on a bumper sticker, it doesn't hold up when life falls apart.

We've created a culture where joy is expected to be the default setting, and suffering feels like something to be hidden. We subtly—and sometimes not so subtly—send the message that real faith can't coexist with sorrow or doubt. If you're walking through pain, you're told to pray harder, believe more, or fake it until you feel it. Talking about your struggles can make you feel like a spiritual buzzkill, as if your honesty might tarnish the carefully polished image of what church is supposed to look like.

So, we learn to wear masks. We walk into church with plastered-on smiles, hiding the grief, anxiety, or anger that's threatening to break us apart. We sing songs about joy unspeakable while choking back tears, afraid that if we let anyone see the cracks, we'll be labeled as faithless or "not spiritual enough." We've made church a place for the already fine, not the broken.

The Church needs a theology that gives us permission to grieve, question, and wrestle. We need a space where it's okay to admit that we don't have all the answers and that sometimes life hurts more than we can bear. We need a faith that can hold the weight of agony, not collapse under it.

This kind of theology doesn't just survive suffering—it transforms it. And it starts by being real, taking off the mask, and allowing the Church to be what it was always meant to be: a hospital for the broken, not a showroom for the perfect.

Let's reclaim the kind of faith that meets people in their suffering, not with shallow platitudes or forced smiles, but with the deep, unshakable hope of Christ. Let's remember that it's okay not to be okay—and that God's love meets us there. Suffering will come—it's as certain as sparks flying upward. The question is, how will we respond? Will our faith hold, or will it crumble?

Getting Honest

Before we go any further, I want to encourage you to pause for a moment. The things we've been discussing deserve space to be wrestled with, not just skimmed over.

Take a breath. Be honest with yourself. These questions aren't about finding the "right" answers; they're about reflecting on where you are right now. Don't rush through them or feel like you need to clean up your thoughts before coming to them. Let this be a space where you can meet God, even in the messy, unpolished parts of your heart.

Grab a journal or your phone, or just sit quietly and take some time to reflect. Let your answers be real. This is where the real work begins.

- What do you believe about suffering?
  How has your life experience shaped your view of God and suffering?

- Have you ever felt pressure to hide your pain or struggles at church?
  Why do you think that is? How has it impacted your faith journey?

- What does "authentic faith" mean to you?
  Can you imagine a version of faith that includes honesty about suffering?

- Think of a time when you wore a "mask" in a church setting.
  What were you afraid of? What would it have felt like, to be honest in that moment?

- When have you felt closest to God in your life?
  Was it during a joyful season or a painful one? What does that tell you about God's presence in suffering?

- What kind of theology of suffering have you absorbed—whether intentionally or unintentionally?
  Does it feel strong enough to sustain you in hard times? If not, what would a stronger theology look like?

- How do you think God feels about your suffering?
  Do you see him as distant, present, indifferent, or compassionate? Why?

The Good Book

When my wife and I first got married, we were determined to start our life together on the right foot. We wanted to honor God as best as we could, and one of our ideas was to read the Bible together before bed each night. I'd heard stories about how my grandparents used to do this, and I thought, What a beautiful way to build a strong foundation for our marriage.

So, we dove right in, deciding to start in the Old Testament—you know, tackle it from the beginning. We picked the book of Judges. Seemed like a solid choice, right? Well...let me tell you, it didn't take long for us to realize this might not have been the best book to wind down with before bed. The part about the woman being chopped up into pieces? Yeah, that was enough to make us slam the brakes (Judges 19).

I honestly hadn't read through Judges in a while, and both of us were stunned by just how violent and dark those chapters were. Every page felt like it was dripping with chaos and brutality. Let's just say we decided to leave Judges and the other Old Testament bloodbaths for daytime reading and moved on to something a little more uplifting for our evenings.

Lesson learned: not all bedtime stories are created equal!

The Bible is, in many ways, a book of suffering. From its opening chapters to its final pages, it tells the stories of humanity's brokenness, pain, and loss. Yet, woven throughout these stories is a thread of hope—an assurance that God is present in the suffering and is working toward ultimate restoration.

Bad Beginnings

The story of suffering begins in the Garden of Eden (Genesis 3). Adam and Eve's disobedience brings sin into the world, introducing pain, toil, and death. The harmonious relationship between humanity and God is fractured, and the consequences ripple through all creation. Eve's childbirth will now be marked by pain, and Adam's work by sweat and struggle. Their exile from Eden is the first great loss humanity experiences—paradise lost.

The suffering deepens with Cain and Abel (Genesis 4). Driven by jealousy, Cain murders his brother, Abel, marking the first recorded act of violence. Abel's blood cries out from the ground, and Cain is condemned to a life of wandering. The first human family learned all too quickly the personal and relational devastation that sin causes.

Sarah's maidservant Hagar is caught in a web of power and pain. She bears Abraham's child, Ishmael, but is mistreated by Sarah and eventually cast out into the wilderness with her son. In her desperation, God meets her, providing water and reassurance (Genesis 16; 21:8-21). Hagar's story highlights the suffering of those pushed to the margins, yet it also demonstrates that God sees and cares for the rejected and the hurting.

Joseph's life is marked by suffering: betrayed by his jealous brothers, sold into slavery, falsely accused of assault, and left to languish in prison. Yet through it all, God is with Joseph, using his suffering to position him to save his family and an entire nation during a famine (Genesis 37-50). Joseph's story illustrates how God can redeem even the darkest circumstances for His purposes.

The Israelites' centuries-long oppression in Egypt epitomizes collective suffering (Exodus 1-12). Enslaved, beaten, and dehumanized, they cry out to God for deliverance. Their suffering becomes the backdrop for God's intervention as He leads them out of bondage with a mighty hand. The Exodus shows both the depth of human suffering and the lengths God will go to bring freedom.

David's life is a tapestry of joy and anguish. As a young shepherd, he defeats Goliath and rises to become Israel's greatest king. Yet his reign is marred by personal failures and devastating losses. His affair with Bathsheba and the resulting death of their child, the rebellion of his son Absalom, and the betrayal by close friends bring David to his knees (1 & 2 Samuel). The psalms, many of which are attributed to him, overflow with cries of lament, showing a heart laid bare before God.

Despite his wisdom, Solomon's later years were marked by idolatry and oppression. His building projects placed heavy burdens on the people, and his worship of foreign gods set the stage for the kingdom's division after his death (1 Kings 11–12). The once-united Israel fractured into two kingdoms—Israel in the north and Judah in the south—both of which would endure centuries of instability and suffering under kings who often "did evil in the sight of the Lord."

The northern kingdom of Israel, in particular, saw a

succession of wicked rulers, including Ahab and Jezebel, whose reigns were marked by idolatry, corruption, and the persecution of God's prophets (1 Kings 16–22). Their rebellion against God led to drought, famine, and eventual conquest by the Assyrians, who brutally destroyed the kingdom and scattered its people (2 Kings 17).

Judah had some righteous kings like Hezekiah and Josiah but was not immune to suffering brought on by its rulers' sins. Kings like Manasseh and Jehoiakim led the nation into deep idolatry, injustice, and violence. Manasseh's reign, described as one of the most evil in Judah's history, included child sacrifice and desecration of the temple (2 Kings 21). His actions provoked God's judgment, ultimately leading to Judah's defeat and exile at the hands of the Babylonians (2 Kings 25).

The prophets often bore the weight of their calling through deep personal suffering. Jeremiah, the "weeping prophet," faced ridicule, imprisonment, and threats to his life as he delivered God's unpopular messages of judgment. Ezekiel was told not to mourn the death of his wife as a sign to Israel. Isaiah foresaw the suffering of the Messiah and endured the rejection of his warnings. The prophetic calling placed these men and women in opposition to the prevailing powers, cultures, and even their communities. The burden of their message—often one of judgment, repentance, and hope—frequently came at great personal cost.

The ultimate story of suffering in the Bible is found in Jesus, the Son of God. From His birth in a humble stable to His betrayal, torture, and crucifixion, Jesus experienced the full depth of human pain. He wept over Jerusalem, mourned the death of His friend Lazarus, and felt the agony of abandonment on the cross.

The New Testament is filled with accounts of the early church enduring persecution. The first martyr, Stephen, is stoned to death for proclaiming the gospel (Acts 7). Paul, imprisoned multiple times, describes beatings, shipwrecks, and constant danger in his letters (2 Corinthians 11:23-28). The apostles and early Christians faced suffering with remarkable courage, believing that their trials were part of sharing in Christ's sufferings.

But suffering is never the final word. Throughout Scripture, God is at work in the middle of pain, loss, and devastation—redeeming, restoring, and rewriting the story. Hagar thought she was abandoned, but God saw her. Joseph was betrayed, but God positioned him for something greater. The Israelites were oppressed, but God delivered them. Even the exile and the cross weren't the end of the story. No matter how dark things get, God is still moving, and suffering doesn't get the last say—He does.

What's In A Name?

The Bible doesn't sugarcoat suffering. It faces it head-on, showing the pain of sin, the consequences of human choices, and the cost of living in a broken world. But it also shows us a God who sees, hears, and enters into our suffering—a God who promises that pain is not the end of the story.

One of the Bible's most famous and deeply profound examples of suffering is, of course, the story of Job. (You knew this was coming.) His unimaginable pain and loss are laid out in the book that bears his name. And even his name gives us a glimpse of what's coming.

The name Job in the Hebrew language is layered with meaning, much like the story it introduces. Scholars have debated its origins and significance, offering several interpretations that reflect the complexity of Job's journey and the weight of his suffering.

The most traditional understanding, derived from the root 'yv (בִּיָא), means "to be hostile" or "to treat as an enemy." This aligns with Job's narrative, where he is seemingly "hated" or "opposed" by his circumstances, Satan, and even, in his perception, by God.

Some scholars suggest the name could be linked to the verb shuv (בוּשׁ), meaning "to return" or "to repent." This interpretation focuses on the ending of Job's story, where he humbles himself and acknowledges God's sovereignty, symbolizing a return to trust and faith despite his suffering.

Another theory connects Iyyov to an older, perhaps pre-Hebrew root that might mean, "Where is the (Divine) Father?" This interpretation reflects Job's spiritual struggle and the book's central question: "Where is God in my suffering?"

Some scholars propose that Job's name has Akkadian roots. The name Ayabba, which resembles Iyyov, appears in ancient Mesopotamian texts and might mean "Where is the divine father?" or "One who cries out." This ties Job's name to the broader ancient Near Eastern traditions of lament and theodicy, showing that his story fits into a larger cultural context of grappling with suffering.

There's also the possibility that Job's name is intentionally mysterious, reflecting his story's ambiguity and unanswered questions. Much like the book itself resists easy answers, the name may invite readers to wrestle with its meaning, just as Job wrestled with his suffering and relationship with God.

Whatever the precise meaning, the name Job is deeply symbolic. It reflects his role as a representative of humanity's struggle with suffering, justice, and faith. Job's story is not just about his pain; it's about the universal human experience of wrestling with the mysteries of life and God's role in it.

Ashes And No Answers

The Book of Job opens by vividly depicting the man at the center of this extraordinary story. It doesn't just tell us his name; it gives us a snapshot of his character, his wealth, and his reputation:

> *In the land of Uz there lived a man whose name was Job. This man was blameless and upright; he feared God and shunned evil. He had seven sons and three daughters, and he owned seven thousand sheep, three thousand camels, five hundred yoke of oxen and five hundred donkeys, and had a large number of servants. He was the greatest man among all the people of the East.*
> Job 1:1-3 NIV

Job wasn't just a good man—he was the man, the kind of person everyone admired. His character was impeccable;

he was described as "blameless and upright," a man who feared God and actively avoided evil. On top of that, Job was wealthy beyond imagination. Seven thousand sheep, three thousand camels, five hundred yoke of oxen, five hundred donkeys, and a vast household of servants—it's the biblical equivalent of being on the Forbes list. And if that weren't enough, he was also a family man, blessed with seven sons and three daughters.

Job's status as "the greatest man among all the people of the East" tells us he wasn't just wealthy and righteous—he was respected. In his time and culture, Job would have been seen as the picture of success, someone who had it all: faith, family, fortune, and favor.

Yet, this setup isn't just an introduction; it's a crucial part of the story. The opening verses of Job set the stage for one of the most profound and challenging explorations of suffering in human history. Why? Because Job's story challenges one of our most ingrained assumptions: that suffering is always a result of sin or poor choices.

If anyone could have avoided suffering based on their behavior, it was Job. He was blameless—not perfect, but morally upright and faithful to God. Yet, despite his righteousness, Job is about to face a series of devastating losses that will leave him broken and questioning everything he thought he knew.

This forces us to grapple with a surprising truth: suffering is not always tied to our actions. Job's story dismantles the simplistic idea that bad things only happen to bad people. Instead, it confronts the reality that even the most faithful can experience profound pain.

It asks us to look beyond the surface and wrestle with deeper questions: Why do the righteous suffer? Where is God in their pain? And how do we reconcile suffering with faith in a good and just God? Job's story invites us to sit with the discomfort, to enter into the mystery of suffering, and to wrestle with the same questions he faced.

Here's where the story takes a shocking and almost unsettling turn—a scene that is both baffling and deeply challenging:

> *One day the angels came to present themselves before the Lord, and Satan also came with them. The Lord said to Satan, 'Where have you come from?'*
>
> *Satan answered the Lord, 'From roaming throughout the earth, going back and forth on it.'*
>
> *Then the Lord said to Satan, 'Have you considered my servant Job? There is no one on earth like him; he is blameless and upright, a man who fears God and shuns evil.' 'Does Job fear God for nothing?' Satan replied. 'Have you not put a hedge around him and his household and everything he has? You have blessed the work of his hands, so that his flocks and herds are spread throughout the land. But now stretch out your hand and strike everything he has, and he will surely curse you to your face.'*
>
> *The Lord said to Satan, 'Very well, then, everything he has is in your power, but on the man himself do not*

> *lay a finger.' Then Satan went out from the presence of the Lord.*

Job 1:6-12 NIV

This scene is nothing short of perplexing. First, we are introduced to a heavenly council—a gathering of angels, or sons of God, in the presence of the Lord. And among them, unexpectedly, is Satan himself.

Dr. Michael Heiser has an interesting take on the opening chapters of Job, particularly about "the satan" who shows up in this heavenly council. In the original Hebrew, the word *satan* has a definite article in front of it—"the satan"—which means it's more of a title than a proper name. So, instead of thinking of this figure as Satan in the sense we often picture him, Heiser points out that "the satan" functions more like a role, something like a prosecuting attorney in God's divine council.

This changes how we might read the scene. Instead of a cosmic embodiment of evil waging war against God, "the satan" is doing a job—testing and challenging human faithfulness. Heiser explains that this adversary is permitted to act within boundaries God sets. God's still in control, but He allows the testing to demonstrate something bigger, namely Job's genuine righteousness and faith that isn't dependent on material blessings.

Now, here's where things get even more uncomfortable. God permits this test, not because Job did anything wrong, but because Job's faithfulness under suffering will reveal something profound about the nature of true righteousness. It's unsettling, sure, but it's also a theme we see over and over in Scripture: trusting God's wisdom even when His ways don't make sense to us.

This perspective challenges us to look at Job with fresh eyes, not just as a personal story of suffering but as part of a bigger framework—a heavenly council with roles, responsibilities, and purposes we might never fully grasp. It's a reminder that our understanding of suffering, justice, and God's sovereignty is always limited.

For us, this passage is hard to swallow. It raises tough questions about God's role in suffering. Why does He permit it? Why doesn't He intervene? And perhaps most hauntingly: Is God complicit in the pain we experience?

What we do see, however, is a God who is not indifferent to suffering. By allowing this test, God doesn't abandon Job—He remains present throughout the ordeal, even if His presence isn't always felt. God's purposes, while mysterious, are ultimately good and redemptive.

Let's not shy away from the discomfort this passage brings. It's okay to feel unsettled, to wrestle with the questions it raises. Job's story challenges us to sit with our doubts and confront them honestly, leading us toward a faith that goes deeper—a faith that doesn't depend on easy answers but remains steadfast, even in the face of uncertainty.

I've listened to countless sermons and poured over many commentaries on this passage. I've come across some insightful points and intriguing perspectives, but if I'm honest, none of them fully satisfy me. I'm still left with lingering questions that don't have easy answers.

It's easy to get stuck on God's role in this whole situation, questioning why He allowed it in the first place. Or

I could go to the other extreme and fixate on the level of freedom the enemy seems to have over Job's life—and, by extension, mine. But, and I think this is the heart of the book, the real focus should be on Job's response. What Job learns through his suffering is what we're meant to take away from his story.

Misery Loves Miserable Advice

When Job's friends—Eliphaz, Bildad, and Zophar—show up, they start off strong. For seven days, they sit silently with Job, grieving alongside him (Job 2:11–13). It's a beautiful picture of solidarity, of simply being there for someone who's suffering. But when they finally open their mouths, things go downhill fast.

Each friend offers a version of the same flawed argument: Job must have done something wrong to deserve this. Eliphaz appeals to his own mystical experience and suggests that Job's suffering is proof of guilt (Job 4:7–8). Bildad is blunt, claiming Job's children probably sinned and got what they deserved (Job 8:3–6). And then there's Zophar—he goes straight for the jugular, saying Job should be grateful his punishment isn't worse (Job 11:6).

Their words reflect an oversimplified view of God and suffering, one where every hardship is neatly explained as punishment for sin. Instead of comforting Job, they heap more pain on him, completely missing the mark. Let's not forget his wife's helpful little gem of advice: "Why don't you just curse God and die?" Sheesh.

A Fresh Perspective

In Job 32, a new voice enters the conversation—a young man named Elihu, who has been silently listening to the debate between Job and his friends but now steps in, frustrated with everyone's failure to address Job's situation properly:

> *But now, Job, listen to my words;*
> *pay attention to everything I say.*
> *I am about to open my mouth;*
> *my words are on the tip of my tongue.*
> *My words come from an upright heart;*
> *my lips sincerely speak what I know.*
>
> Job 33:1-3 NIV

He is one of the more mysterious figures in Job's story. He's the youngest of the group, and, honestly, he comes off a bit intense. He doesn't just critique Job's friends for failing to answer Job properly—he goes after Job himself, accusing him of speaking out of turn about God and questioning His justice.

Now, Elihu's speeches are polarizing. Some theologians have praised him as a voice of divine wisdom over the centuries, while others have written him off as an arrogant, overzealous youth. Even today, scholars debate whether his speeches were part of the original text of Job or added later. But here's the thing: no ancient manuscript of Job excludes Elihu. He's there in every version we've got. And what's more, while God rebukes Job's three friends at the end of the story, He never rebukes Elihu. That silence is telling.

Elihu brings something different to the table. While Job's friends cling to their tired "retribution theology"—the idea that suffering is always a direct result of sin—Elihu challenges that. He doesn't say Job's suffering is punishment for some hidden sin, but he does point out that Job's words, born out of his pain, have crossed a line. Job has started justifying himself at God's expense, and Elihu isn't having it.

> *So listen to me, you men of understanding.*
> *Far be it from God to do evil,*
> *from the Almighty to do wrong.*
> *He repays everyone for what they have done;*
> *he brings on them what their conduct deserves.*
> *It is unthinkable that God would do wrong,*
> *that the Almighty would pervert justice.*

Job 34:10-12 NIV

Elihu strongly rejects the notion that Job's suffering compromises God's goodness while dismissing the idea that Job's hardship is a punishment for sin. So, is it God's fault or Job's fault? Neither. Elihu says to Job:

> *But you have said in my hearing—I heard the very words—'I am pure, I have done no wrong; I am clean and free from sin. Yet God has found fault with me; he considers me his enemy.' But I tell you, in this you are not right, for God is greater than any mortal.*

Job 33:8-12 NIV

Elihu acknowledges Job's claim of innocence and does not accuse him of hidden sin like the other friends. Instead, he reframes the suffering as a tool God uses for purposes beyond human understanding. Elihu explains:

> *But those who suffer he delivers in their suffering; he speaks to them in their affliction. He is wooing you from the jaws of distress to a spacious place free from restriction, to the comfort of your table laden with choice food.*
>
> Job 36:15-16 NIV

Elihu suggests that God uses suffering to instruct, refine, and deliver rather than to punish.

What stands out in Elihu's speeches is his emphasis on God's greatness. He reminds Job—and us—that God's ways are far beyond our understanding. Our righteousness or sin doesn't alter God's character, but it deeply affects us and those around us. Elihu's speeches are like a prelude to God's thunderous entrance later in the story. He shifts the focus back where it belongs—not on Job's suffering or his unanswered questions, but on the sovereignty and goodness of God.

Elihu's words remind us that when we're tempted to shake our fists at the heavens in our darkest moments, we might need to pause and consider just how vast, wise, and good God really is.

The Creator Speaks

When God finally speaks (Job 38–41), He doesn't offer the kind of answers Job was hoping for. Instead, God responds with a series of questions that convey the vastness of His wisdom and power. He talks about creating the earth, setting the boundaries of the seas, and controlling the stars and the weather. He describes wild beasts that live beyond human control and understanding.

Here's the thing: God doesn't directly address Job's suffering. He doesn't explain why it happened. Instead, He shifts the focus from Job's pain to God's greatness. It's as if God is saying, "You may not understand everything, but trust Me—I've got this."

And just in case we're tempted to side with Job's friends, God shuts that down, too. He rebukes them for misrepresenting Him and praises Job for speaking honestly (Job 42:7–8). God values Job's raw, unfiltered wrestling far more than the shallow, tidy answers his friends tried to offer.

After hearing God's response, Job humbles himself. He admits he spoke of things he didn't understand and confesses the limits of his own perspective (Job 42:3). Job's repentance isn't about sin that caused his suffering—it's about realizing that his understanding of God was too small.

Job doesn't get all the answers he wants, but he finds something better: a deeper trust in the God who was with him through it all.

What We Learn From Job

Don't Be Like Job's Friends. Job's friends remind us that oversimplified theology—trying to explain suffering with easy answers—can do more harm than good. Sometimes, the best thing you can do is just sit with someone in their pain and keep your mouth shut.

God Can Handle Your Questions. Job's honesty, even when it bordered on accusing God, wasn't condemned. If anything, it brought him closer to God. Don't be afraid to wrestle with your doubts and questions—they're part of a real relationship with Him.

God's Perspective Is Bigger Than Ours. God's response shows us that there's so much we don't see or understand. While we might not get the answers we want, we can trust that God's wisdom and plans are far beyond anything we can imagine.

Restoration Doesn't Erase Pain. In the end, God restores Job's fortunes and gives him a new family (Job 42:10–17). But let's be real—nothing could fully undo the losses Job experienced. Restoration doesn't mean pretending the pain never happened; it means that God can bring beauty and purpose out of it.

Job's story doesn't wrap suffering up in a tidy package with all the answers we want. But at its heart, Job's story is about faith—a faith that doesn't depend on having everything figured out but instead leans on the God who stays with us, even in the storm.

A Hymn Born From Heartbreak

Horatio Spafford's story is one of unimaginable loss transformed into a timeless message of faith and hope. A successful lawyer and businessman in 19th-century Chicago, Spafford seemed to have it all—wealth, a thriving career, and a beautiful family. But his life took a tragic turn, marked by one devastating blow after another.

In 1871, the Great Chicago Fire destroyed much of Spafford's real estate investments, wiping out a significant portion of his wealth. Even as he worked to recover financially, his personal life would be shaken even more deeply. In 1873, Spafford planned a trip to Europe for his wife, Anna, and their four daughters to provide a much-needed break after their hardships. Business obligations delayed his departure, so he sent his family ahead on the *SS Ville du Havre* ocean liner.

Tragically, the ship collided with another vessel in the middle of the Atlantic. Within minutes, the *Ville du Havre* sank. Anna survived, clinging to a piece of debris, but all four of their daughters—Annie, Maggie, Bessie, and Tanetta—were lost. Anna sent her husband a brief but haunting telegram: "Saved alone."

Grieving and heartbroken, Spafford immediately set sail to join his wife. During the voyage, as his ship passed near the spot where his daughters had drowned, he penned the words to the hymn *It Is Well with My Soul*.

The hymn is a remarkable expression of faith amid profound sorrow. Its opening lines reflect both his grief and his unshakable trust in God:

When peace like a river attendeth my way,
When sorrows like sea billows roll;
Whatever my lot, Thou hast taught me to say,
It is well, it is well with my soul.

Horatio and Anna Spafford went on to rebuild their lives. They moved to Jerusalem and founded a Christian community that focused on serving the poor and disadvantaged. Horatio Spafford's life reminds us that suffering doesn't have the final word. His hymn, born out of tragedy, has become a source of comfort for millions. It reflects the tension we all experience between pain and hope, between despair and trust.

It Is Well with My Soul is more than a hymn; it's a reminder that even in our deepest grief, we can find peace in the presence of the One who carries us through.

Ashley's Story

Alex and I met at 18, quickly fell in love, and knew we wanted to serve the Lord together for the rest of our lives. We got engaged at 22, married at 23, and became pregnant at 24. At the time, we were serving in college ministry, where our faith had deepened during our own years in school.

But we sensed a shift, and at eight months pregnant, God moved us to Savannah to help launch The Dwelling Church. The Lord gave us promises and words to hold onto, making this transition feel like an act of obedience. We named our son Aiden, meaning "fiery one." Before we left, our community prayed over me as the song New Wine played: *"I lay down my old flame to carry your new fire today."* Holding my belly, I knew the Lord was doing something new.

But I wasn't prepared for how difficult the transition would be. Aiden was an amazing little boy, but parenting him felt harder than it did for others. He was discontent and intensely defiant. As he grew, he lost language and social interaction. Being a mom had been my lifelong dream, but I felt like I was failing.

When I was three months pregnant with our daughter, Iley, I took two-and-a-half-year-old Aiden for a psychological evaluation. After six exhausting hours, I heard the words: *"Your son has autism. The gap between him and his peers will only grow larger."* Wrestling him into his car seat, I broke down. *What does this mean? Can he live a happy and full life? Will our family be okay?*

Following his diagnosis, Aiden's struggles only intensified—constant screaming, biting, spitting, tics, destruction, vocalizations, being awake all through the night stimming, debilitating OCD, self-injury, no sense of safety, inability to communicate, inability to follow instructions, aggression toward his sister and others, eloping, inappropriate and uncontrollable laughter, constant meltdowns, defiance, taking his clothes off, compulsions, and intense fears.

There were seasons when he refused to be indoors, spat and peed on everything, ran into roads, and, for an entire year, could not share a room with or even hear his sister's voice. We became isolated, as it became necessary to turn down every invitation and step away from ministry and community. Our days were so dark that we went months at a time without a single moment of pleasure or even neutrality. It was pure distress and crisis around the clock.

I would weep every single day and all through the nights, and at my lowest, all I could pray was a whispered and weak, *"Jesus, have mercy."* I'd leave the house and feel like a stranger in conversations, crying on the way back home from profound loneliness. We were in chronic survival mode, wondering why God hadn't stepped in but still believing for a miracle. I threw myself into research, prayed (begged) for healing, took communion daily, and sought every therapy and medical option available. But despite everything, every single month was worse than the one before—for years. And not once did we ever see Aiden himself as the struggle—my heartbreak was driven by seeing my son seemingly hidden behind immense suffering, and not being able to help him. It was unbearable, and grief consumed every single corner of our life.

How could we pray so hard, yet things only get worse? I wrestled deeply with my identity, feeling as though the promises of God over my life and my own dreams were dead, buried under our reality. It felt like the enemy was winning, and I had been abandoned by God. I wanted so badly to remain in a place of great faith, but my heart was shattered, angry, and full of questions.

Why did this happen to Aiden? Why does it feel like our prayers aren't doing anything? Is my faith too weak? If his healing depends on me, how cruel would that be when I'm already so broken? Even in my questioning, I felt deep conviction for my bitterness.

Scripture makes it clear that we will have trouble and heartbreak in this world, and I realized—if this trial could drive me away from Jesus, then my faith had always been conditional. Was my love for God based on Him meeting my expectations? If my yes became bitter in struggle, was it ever truly a yes? Was my hope in Jesus or in a certain outcome?

As I wrestled with God, I nailed down a few truths in my heart:

- God is who He says He is.
- God did not give Aiden autism or send a trial to our family to teach us a lesson.
- It is God's will to heal.
- It grieves the heart of God to see His children suffer.
- God does not withhold good things because of our weakness.

The only way I could move forward was by becoming more comfortable with mystery. I started focusing on what I knew to be true about God rather than what I didn't understand about our circumstances. Fixing my eyes on Him humbled, centered, and strengthened me. But I still had so much grief, anger, and disappointment to sort through. So, I just chose to grieve in His presence and ask Him to help my unbelief.

One night, I needed to get out of the house and cry, so I grabbed crackers and juice for communion and took a drive. As I wept, a guttural scream came out of me, and I realized—*this is prayer*. Grief doesn't have to pull us away from worship; it can be worship if we turn our hearts toward Him in the midst of it. It doesn't have to be pretty; it just has to be honest. I wanted a genuine faith, and I knew there was no way out but through.

I took communion, pleading the blood of Jesus over my family and reminding myself of Jesus' sacrifice and my covenant relationship with the God who loves Aiden more than I do. And I felt His grief over what Aiden and our family were going through, and His desire to be near. This shift—seeing His heartbreak and nearness—helped me trust His heart for Aiden again.

I just kept worshipping. The strength and peace I felt after being in His presence—without an agenda, just pure exaltation—were the only moments that made me feel like we were going to be okay. He reminded me of His nature as He sat with me at my lowest, then picked me up to keep walking. Self-preservation and self-satisfaction were slowly squeezed out of my worship, and I have grown to love the sacrifice of worshipping in pain simply because He deserves it.

Our struggles felt like they were going to crush me, but He actually used them to further shape me into His image and give me peace that's not tethered to the outcome. I am so grateful for all that has been formed in me in this season. He has made connection more valuable to me than self-sufficiency, and I've seen what a community can look like when we allow ourselves to depend on each other. He has developed patience, endurance, sacrifice, self-control, and faith in me through this refining fire. He has sustained my marriage. He has deepened my empathy and sensitivity to others' suffering. He is dismantling my desire to prove myself or be understood. He has increased my confidence as I have settled more into who I want to be, and increased my boldness as I have learned how to advocate for my children. He has brought me back to a place of immense awe and gratitude for the gospel and my salvation. He has, and is, teaching me how to wait. He has always given my husband and I clarity and peace in our decisions, from ideas and strategies in parenting to knowing which doctors to trust. I could go on and on. The Lord has been so faithful to our family and we have seen His miracle working power in our life and in Aiden's mind and body. We are not where we were, and I'm confident we are also not where we'll end up.

Miraculously, after a year of separation, Aiden became okay with being around his sister Iley, and now we are able to do things as a family of four again. Playing in the backyard, going on walks, sitting at the dinner table together— it all feels euphoric. I'm grateful for the simplicity of joy we are experiencing. Aiden is beginning to communicate more, initiate play with Iley and other children, thrive in school, sleep through the night, and has such a happy, goofy, and affectionate demeanor. He is wonderful and exceptional and so insanely loved.

I am reminded again of the lyrics sung over me while pregnant with Aiden, but with so much more meaning now: *"In the crushing, in the pressing, You are making new wine. In the soil, I now surrender, You are breaking new ground."* Even though we still have discouraging and difficult moments, I see the hand of God all over our life, and I've decided in my heart that I trust Him. I still have faith that the Lord will continue bringing Aiden to a place of healing and fullness. But I don't wait on any one thing as my only way forward anymore. Jesus is my way, here and now.

In this you greatly rejoice, though now for a little while you have been grieved by various trials, that the genuineness of your faith...may be found to praise, honor, and glory at the
revelation of Jesus Christ.

1 Peter 1:6-9

CHAPTER THREE

MYTHS ABOUT SUFFERING

As a pastor, I've had countless conversations with people grappling with suffering, and one thing I've noticed is how easily myths about suffering creep into our thinking. These myths pop up in the words of those in the middle of trials, desperately trying to make sense of their pain. I hear them in the well-meaning advice of friends or family members trying to offer comfort. And, if I'm completely honest, I've believed some of these myths myself. Worse yet, I've even perpetuated them from time to time—thinking I was being helpful, only to realize later how incomplete or untrue those sentiments were.

These myths about suffering tend to grow out of our discomfort with pain and our desire to tidy up what is messy. After all, we want suffering to make sense. We want it to have a clear cause and a quick solution. But the reality of suffering is rarely so straightforward. The myths we cling to often reveal more about our fears and limitations than they do about God's purposes. Yet they persist—shaping how we view God, ourselves, and the world around us in ways that can ultimately do more harm than good.

That's why it's so important to confront them honestly and examine them through the lens of Scripture and truth. Because when we cling to these myths, we not only distort the nature of suffering—we risk distorting the character of God Himself. And personally, that's a risk I'm no longer willing to take.

Let's look at some of the most believable myths around suffering and dismantle them. They might seem comforting or even logical initially, but when real pain shows up, they just don't hold up.

Myth: Suffering Is God's Punishment

It's a question that slips into the back of our minds when life turns upside down: *Is God punishing me?* We've all been there—replaying mistakes, revisiting regrets, and wondering if our suffering is somehow the result of divine payback. Maybe it's because of that unwise decision we made years ago or the words we wish we could take back. Maybe it's because we think we haven't prayed enough, haven't read the Bible enough, or haven't been "good enough." The thought sneaks in during the quiet moments, planting seeds of doubt about God's goodness and intentions.

I recently heard someone say, "I think God might be punishing me," as they worked through a painful relationship issue. And honestly, I get it. When life feels unbearable, it's easy to assume God must be evening the score, doling out punishment for something in our past. But this assumption says more about how we see God than about who He truly is. It paints a picture of a God who's harsh and vindictive, keeping a ledger of our mistakes, rather than a God full of love and compassion.

Here's the truth we need to hold onto: *God is good. Always good.*

Scripture tells us He is love (1 John 4:8), and everything He does flows from that love. Even when we experience the consequences of our choices—what the Bible calls "reaping what you sow" (Galatians 6:7-8)—it's not about God punishing us. God's discipline, when it comes, isn't about causing pain for pain's sake. It's about shaping, teaching, and drawing us closer to Him.

Consequences aren't the same as punishment. We live in a world of cause and effect. If you spend recklessly, you may find yourself in financial difficulty. If you hurt someone with your words or actions, it may damage the relationship. These are natural consequences, not divine punishments. God doesn't need to "punish" us when our choices naturally lead to hardship. That's just how the world works.

But God doesn't leave us to wallow in the mess we've made. Instead, He steps into the situation with us, offering grace and wisdom to help us grow. He's not waiting to smite us for every misstep. He's working to redeem even our worst mistakes for His glory and our good (Romans 8:28).

So, how can we be sure God is not punishing us? It's easy to assume that suffering equals punishment, but that's not how God operates. Here are a few truths to remember when you're struggling:

God's Discipline is Loving, Not Vindictive. Hebrews 12:6 reminds us that "the Lord disciplines the one he loves." Discipline is not the same as punishment. Discipline is corrective and redemptive; punishment is retributive. God's discipline, when it comes, is always rooted in His love for us, aimed at helping us grow and stay close to Him.

God's Justice and Mercy Converged at the Cross. Jesus took on the consequences of sin and its brokenness (Isaiah 53:5), offering Himself to reconcile humanity and God. This profound act assures us that our suffering is not divine retribution—Jesus' sacrifice fully addressed the divide caused by sin. Instead, our suffering reflects the reality of living in a fallen world, where pain and difficulty persist, even as God works to redeem all things.

Not all Suffering is Personal. Some suffering is simply the result of living in a fallen world. Disease, natural disasters, and systemic injustice aren't about you personally. They're part of the brokenness that entered the world through sin. God's plan is to redeem and restore, but we're not there yet. Until then, we live in the tension of a beautiful and broken world.

God is More Interested in Redemption than Retribution. The story of the Bible isn't about God punishing humanity—it's about God rescuing humanity. Even in our pain, He's working to redeem us, to bring good out of what feels like senseless suffering. That's His heart. That's who

He is.

So, if you're reading this and you've feared that God's punishment is directed toward you, here's some good news to hold onto. This truth offers profound comfort when we're wrestling with the idea that God might be punishing us in our suffering:

> *There is no fear in love. But perfect love drives out fear, because fear has to do with punishment. The one who fears is not made perfect in love.*
>
> 1 John 4:18 NIV

John is telling us this: fear of punishment doesn't belong in the life of someone who has encountered God's perfect love. Through Christ, God's love has already made a way for us. Jesus bore the weight of sin and its consequences, so punishment is no longer on the table for those who are in Him. Suffering, while painful and confusing, is not about God's wrath or penalty.

When we face suffering and fear that God might be punishing us, this verse invites us to reframe our understanding of God's actions. Punishment is rooted in judgment and condemnation, but love is rooted in relationship and redemption. God's perfect love has cast out the fear of punishment for those who belong to Him. Whatever we're enduring, we can trust that it's not about God's anger but about His presence with us.

So, how do we apply this? When fear rises and the question, *"Is God punishing me?"* creeps in, let this verse remind you of the truth. Rest in God's love. Let His perfect love drive out the fear that suffering is some kind of divine payback. Instead, lean into the assurance that God's love is constant, even in hardship. He's not distant or angry—He's near, holding you in His arms of grace and guiding you toward a greater understanding of His heart.

When suffering comes, it's natural to ask, "Why?" The question lingers in the quiet moments, gnawing at our hearts. But before jumping to the conclusion that God is punishing you, take a step back and approach the situation with a clearer view of who God is and how He operates.

Examine Your Heart. Suffering can sometimes be a wake-up call, a way God gets our attention when we drift. But even then, it's not about punishment—it's about loving correction. Think of a parent gently guiding a child back onto the right path, not with harshness, but with care and concern. Ask yourself: Is there something God might be trying to teach me in this season? What part of my life is He refining?

Focus on God's Character. Remember who He has revealed Himself to be—merciful, loving, and slow to anger (Psalm 103:8). This is not a God who delights in your pain or waits for you to fail. He's for you, not against you (Romans 8:31). When you begin to question His motives, remind yourself of His steadfast love and commitment to your good.

Look for God's Presence in the Pain. God doesn't promise us a life free from suffering—far from it. But He does promise to walk with us through it. His presence in your trial may show up as unexpected comfort, provision when you least expect it, or strength to keep going when you thought you couldn't. Watch for those moments, those glimpses of His nearness, even when life feels overwhelming.

Remember the Cross. If you ever doubt God's intentions toward you, remember the cross. The God who gave His life for you isn't the God who's trying to crush you. He's the God who loves you with an everlasting love. The cross is proof that whatever you're facing isn't about retribution—it's about a God who entered into our brokenness to redeem and restore. Suffering may be part of the journey, but punishment is not the final word for those who are in Christ.

Suffering can make us question everything—our choices, our faith, and even God's goodness. But here's what I've learned: God's goodness is our anchor. When life feels chaotic, when the pain is overwhelming, when the questions go unanswered, His character doesn't change. He is good. He is for us. And He is with us, even in our hardships.

So, is God punishing you? If you're in Christ, the answer is no. Jesus took care of that on the cross. What you're experiencing now is not wrath but a world still groaning for redemption. Hold on to that truth, and hold on to Him.

Myth: Suffering Is Always Evidence Of Personal Sin

It's a common assumption, especially in some Christian circles, that suffering must be tied directly to personal sin. The thinking often goes something like this: if you're suffering, it's because you did something to "open the door" to the devil's attacks or God's judgment. I once spoke with a parent of a child with special needs who painfully recounted a conversation where someone had the audacity to suggest that her child's challenges must have been caused by her own sin. The implication was clear: the mother was to blame. Not only is this a glaring example of bad theology, but it's also staggeringly cruel and thoughtless—especially to say such a thing to a grieving parent.

While it's true that sin can have consequences—and that spiritual warfare is real—this perspective oversimplifies suffering and paints a distorted picture of both God and the world He created. Let's dig into this and see what Scripture has to say.

There is biblical support for the idea that sin can lead to suffering. Proverbs 22:8 says, "Whoever sows injustice will reap calamity." Galatians 6:7 reinforces this: "Do not be deceived: God is not mocked, for whatever one sows, that will he also reap." These verses remind us that our choices have real-world consequences, and sin often brings destruction to ourselves and those around us.

In John 5:14, after healing the invalid at the pool of Bethesda, Jesus tells him, "See, you are well again. Stop sinning, or something worse may happen to you." This could indicate that his suffering was tied to sin, or it might simply be a warning about the destructive power of sin in general. Either way, Scripture does affirm that sin can result in hardship, whether through natural consequences or God's loving discipline (Hebrews 12:6).

But here's the thing: while sin can cause suffering, the Bible makes it abundantly clear that not all suffering is a direct result of personal sin. The story of Job dismantles this idea. Job's friends were quick to insist that some hidden sin must have caused his suffering, but God rebuked them in the end, declaring that they spoke wrongly about Him (Job 42:7-8). Job's suffering wasn't a punishment—it was part of a greater spiritual story that Job and his friends couldn't see.

Jesus Himself refutes this thinking in John 9:1-3. When His disciples ask Him about a man born blind, saying, "Rabbi, who sinned, this man or his parents, that he was born blind?" Jesus replies, "Neither this man nor his parents sinned, but this happened so that the works of God might be displayed in him." Jesus makes it clear that not all suffering is tied to sin. Sometimes, it's about God's purposes unfolding in ways we can't immediately understand.

So what about spiritual warfare? The idea that sin "opens the door" for Satan has become a popular explanation in some Christian circles. Ephesians 4:27 warns, "Do not give the devil a foothold," and it's often interpreted to mean that sin creates opportunities for spiritual attack. While there's truth here, it's not the whole story.

First, this perspective can lead to unhealthy fear and self-obsession. Instead of seeing God as sovereign, it frames Satan as a rogue agent with unchecked power. The Bible paints a different picture: Satan can only act within the boundaries God allows, as we see in the opening chapters of Job. This doesn't mean we ignore the reality of spiritual warfare—Ephesians 6:12 reminds us that our struggle is against spiritual forces—but it does mean we place our trust in God's authority, not our ability to "close doors" or perfectly avoid every sin.

Second, this mindset can lead to misplaced guilt. If we

believe every trial or attack is the result of our mistakes, we'll carry an unbearable burden of self-blame. Sin indeed has consequences, but not every hardship is tied to a specific failure. The Bible shows us a God who is not only merciful but also fully in control. We are invited to trust Him, not live in fear of making a misstep that will ruin everything.

But what about the times when suffering really is the result of our actions? What if you're facing the fallout of poor decisions, moral failures, or outright rebellion against God? Here's the good news: your mistakes don't have to define the rest of your life.

The Bible is full of people who messed up—big time—and still found redemption. Think of Peter, who denied Jesus three times but became the rock on which the Church was built. Or Paul, who persecuted Christians before becoming one of the greatest missionaries of all time. Their stories remind us that God's grace is greater than our failures.

If you're suffering because of personal sin, the first step is to own it. Psalm 32:5 says, "Then I acknowledged my sin to you and did not cover up my iniquity. I said, 'I will confess my transgressions to the Lord.' And you forgave the guilt of my sin." Confession and repentance are the pathways to healing. They don't erase the consequences of sin, but they do bring us back into alignment with God's grace and love.

Once you've confessed, let go of the shame. Romans 8:1 reminds us, "There is now no condemnation for those who are in Christ Jesus." God doesn't hold your past over your head, and you don't have to either. You can move forward in forgiveness, trusting that God can take even the messiest parts of your story and use them for good.

Finally, don't tie every trial to your mistakes. Life in a broken world guarantees that we'll face suffering, whether we deserve it or not. Instead of getting stuck in guilt or analyzing every hardship, focus on God's character. He's not a punitive God waiting to strike you down; He's a loving Father who walks with you, redeems your pain, and invites you into freedom.

Here's the takeaway: suffering isn't always about sin.

It's about living in a world that groans for redemption. While it's important to acknowledge when our choices contribute to hardship, we can't let shame keep us from moving forward. God's grace covers us, His sovereignty sustains us, and His presence reminds us that even in our pain, we are never alone. Whether suffering comes from sin, spiritual warfare, or simply the brokenness of life, the path forward is the same: trust in the God who redeems all things for His glory and our good.

Myth: You Don't Have Enough Faith

One of the most pervasive and damaging myths about suffering is the idea that if you're experiencing hardship, it must mean you don't have enough faith. Maybe you haven't prayed hard enough, believed deeply enough, or trusted completely enough. This notion whispers that the pain in your life is somehow your fault, that your lack of faith is holding you back from God's blessings or healing. It's a tempting idea because it gives us the illusion of control: if we just muster up enough faith, we can avoid suffering altogether. But Scripture dismantles this myth at every turn.

Let's look at the Bible's "Hall of Faith" in Hebrews 11. The writer recounts story after story of faithful men and women who trusted God in extraordinary ways. Some saw miraculous deliverance: Noah was saved through the flood, Abraham received his promised son, and the Israelites crossed the Red Sea on dry ground. But the chapter doesn't stop there. It goes on to describe others who were mocked, flogged, imprisoned, stoned, and even killed. It says they were "commended for their faith, yet none of them received what had been promised" (Hebrews 11:39). Faith didn't shield them from suffering. Instead, it sustained them through it.

We see this pattern over and over in Scripture. Paul, one of the most faithful servants of Christ, endured relentless hardship. He was beaten, shipwrecked, imprisoned, and afflicted with a mysterious "thorn in the flesh" that he begged God to remove. God's response? "My grace is sufficient for you, for my power is made perfect in weakness" (2 Corinthians 12:9). Paul's faith didn't remove his suffering, but it gave him the strength to endure, trusting that God's power was at work in his pain.

Even Jesus, the Son of God, experienced suffering despite His perfect faith. In the Garden of Gethsemane, He prayed with such intensity that His sweat fell like drops of blood. "Father, if you are willing, take this cup from me," He pleaded. But then He added, "Yet not my will, but yours be done" (Luke 22:42). Jesus' faith wasn't about avoiding suffering; it was about submitting to God's will, even when that will included the cross.

So, where does that leave us when we pray? How do we reconcile faith-filled prayers with the reality of unanswered or delayed prayers? It's a tension we all feel, and the Bible gives us guidance for navigating it.

Faithful prayer is not about manipulating God into giving us what we want. It's about aligning our hearts with His will. Jesus modeled this in the Lord's Prayer: "Your kingdom come, your will be done, on earth as it is in heaven" (Matthew 6:10). Our prayers should be bold and full of faith, but they should also be rooted in trust that God's will is better than ours.

Think of Shadrach, Meshach, and Abednego standing before King Nebuchadnezzar and his fiery furnace. Their faith was unwavering as they declared, "The God we serve is able to deliver us from the blazing furnace... But even if He does not, we want you to know, Your Majesty, that we will not serve your gods" (Daniel 3:17-18). They trusted in God's power to save them, but their faith wasn't dependent on the outcome.

It's a reminder that faith isn't about the certainty of a particular result; it's about the certainty of who God is. It's trusting in His goodness, even when the answer to our prayer is "not yet" or "not in the way you expect."

But let's be honest—this isn't easy. It's one thing to say "trust God" when life is smooth sailing, but when the storm hits, doubt creeps in. We wonder if our prayers are bouncing off the ceiling or if we've done something wrong to deserve the silence. Here's where we need to anchor ourselves in the truth of God's character.

God isn't silent because He's indifferent or distant. He's not withholding good things because you haven't prayed the "right" way or believed hard enough. He's a good Father who knows what we need, even when we don't understand His timing. Sometimes, He delays because He's working out something deeper in us or around us. Other times, His "no" is a form of protection or preparation for something better. Faith doesn't mean we always understand His ways, but it does mean we trust His heart.

So, how do we keep praying without losing heart? Jesus told a parable about a persistent widow who kept pleading with a judge for justice. Eventually, the judge granted her request, not because he cared about her, but because she wore him down (Luke 18:1-8). Jesus' point wasn't that God is like the judge—it's that we should never give up in prayer. Keep bringing your burdens to Him, not because you're trying to twist His arm, but because prayer keeps you connected to the One who loves you most.

At the same time, we must learn to hold our requests with open hands. Faith isn't a bargaining chip; it's a posture of surrender. It's saying, "God, I trust You to answer this in the way that is best, even if it's not what I expect or want."

Faith calls us to keep praying, keep trusting, and keep walking with God, even when the answers don't come the way we hope. It's not about having everything figured out—it's about trusting the One who does.

A Test For Good Measure

Or maybe you still don't believe me. Maybe you're

hanging onto the idea that your lack of faith is the problem. Let's settle this with a little test. If you're wondering if you've got the kind of faith that should guarantee a suffering-free life, let's find out! (Spoiler: You won't like the results.)

Have you prayed exactly the right number of times today?

If you don't know how many times that is, don't worry—neither does anyone else. But surely it's more than you've prayed so far.

Did you say all the "magic words" in your prayer?

Be sure to include phrases like "hedge of protection" and "claiming victory" or God might not hear you. And don't forget to end with "In Jesus' name," or it doesn't count.

Are you 100% free of doubt at all times?

You can't have even a tiny flicker of doubt. None. Zip. Zero. Perfect confidence, all the time. What do you mean that's impossible?

Do you believe hard enough?

Remember, it's not just about believing—it's about believing harder. Clench your fists, furrow your brow, and really mean it this time.

Have you sinned recently?

No? Great. But are you sure? Have you thought about every unkind word and impure thought or even skipped prayer time? Better double-check—you wouldn't want your suffering to be your fault.

Are you following all the unspoken rules?

You know, the ones nobody tells you about until you've already broken them? Better hope you guessed correctly.

Results:

If you answered "no" to any of these questions, congratulations! You're human. The good news? God's love and grace don't operate on a ridiculous point system.

Let's throw this checklist in the trash where it belongs and remember: faith isn't about perfect performance—it's about trusting a perfect God. Faith isn't a way to avoid suffering; it's what sustains you in the middle of it. So, take a deep breath. God isn't waiting for you to get everything just right—He's already walking with you, no matter where you are.

Myth: Just Suck It Up And Deal With It

We've all heard it—or worse, thought it. Life gets hard, and someone (maybe even you) says, *"Just suck it up. Deal with it. Stop complaining."* It's the rallying cry of independence and grit, but let's be honest—it's also pride masquerading as strength.

When life throws curveballs, "sucking it up" might seem like the noble thing to do. We don't want to burden others with our problems or fear being labeled weak or incapable. But here's the truth: trying to tough it out alone doesn't make you stronger; it just isolates you. You don't need to wear your suffering like some twisted badge of honor, as if ignoring your pain is proof of your faith or your toughness.

Some of us are "fix-it" people. We like to roll up our sleeves, get our hands dirty, and find a solution. There's a certain satisfaction in being able to solve problems and move forward. But what happens when you face something that can't be fixed? What happens when no amount of effort, ingenuity, or determination will change the diagnosis, bring someone back, or undo the damage?

That's when the "fix-it" mindset crumbles. You realize you can't outwork or outthink your way out of this one. And if your identity is built on being the strong, capable one, you're left feeling untethered, adrift in a sea of questions. You wonder, "If I can't fix this, who am I?" That's the trap of relying on your own strength—it will fail you when you need it most.

Trying to bury your struggles doesn't make them go away. Pain doesn't stay buried—it festers. Ignoring your emotions is like trying to hold a beach ball underwater. Sure, you might manage it for a while, but eventually, it will pop up with even more force than before.

When you suppress your pain, it often comes out sideways. You snap at your spouse or kids, withdraw from friends, or spiral into bitterness. Your unresolved hurt starts shaping how you see the world, God, and yourself. Worse, bottling it up isolates you from the people who could help carry your burden. You convince yourself that no one would understand or, worse, that no one cares.

But the Bible is clear: "Bear one another's burdens, and

so fulfill the law of Christ" (Galatians 6:2). You were never meant to carry the weight of suffering on your own. God didn't design you for solitary strength—He designed you for community.

Let me say it plainly: Being honest about your pain doesn't make you weak. It makes you human. Jesus Himself wasn't afraid to be vulnerable. He wept openly when His friend Lazarus died (John 11:35). He prayed in agony in the Garden of Gethsemane, even asking His closest friends to stay awake and support Him in His darkest hour (Matthew 26:38-39). If the Son of God wasn't afraid to show His pain, why are we?

When you admit your struggles—first to yourself, then to God, and then to others—you're not just acknowledging the pain. You're opening the door for healing. You're giving God room to work in the places you've been trying to keep Him out. And you're inviting others to be the hands and feet of Christ in your life.

We need each other. It's as simple as that. God designed us to live in community, to share our joys and struggles. When you let people into your pain, something amazing happens. You discover you're not alone. You realize that other people have been where you are—and that they've made it through. Their stories become a source of hope and encouragement.

Sharing your struggles also strengthens the people around you. Vulnerability breeds vulnerability. When you open up, you give others permission to do the same. You create a space where honesty is welcome, where burdens are shared, and where healing can begin.

But let's be real—inviting others into your pain is risky. Not everyone will respond well. Some people will offer shallow platitudes or try to "fix" you. That's okay. You're not looking for perfect responses; you're looking for presence. True community isn't about having all the right answers—it's about showing up again and again.

Here's the paradox: Real strength isn't about gritting your teeth and pretending everything's fine.

It's about surrender. It's about admitting you can't handle it all and trusting God to carry what you can't. That kind of surrender takes courage. It takes humility. But it's also where the healing begins. When you let go of the need to "just deal with it," you create space for God to move. You start to see His hand in the midst of your pain—His comfort, His provision, His strength. And you discover a strength that's not your own, rooted in His unshakable love and power.

It might mean praying an honest prayer like, "God, I can't do this on my own. I need Your help." It might mean reaching out to a friend, pastor, or counselor and saying, "I'm struggling, and I need someone to talk to." It might mean stepping away from the endless cycle of "fixing" and just sitting in God's presence, letting Him remind you that He's with you.

If you're someone who prides yourself on being able to handle everything, this might feel like a punch to the gut. But hear me out: Asking for help isn't failure. Admitting you're struggling doesn't mean you're weak. It means you're human. And God meets us in our humanity, not in our pretense of strength.

So, the next time you catch yourself thinking, "I just need to suck it up," pause. Take a deep breath. And remember that you don't have to carry this alone. Let God and the people He's placed in your life shoulder the burden with you. That's where true strength lies—in surrender, honesty, and community.

In The Valley With The Prince of Preachers

When we think of great Christian leaders, we often imagine people whose faith allowed them to rise above life's difficulties easily. Charles Spurgeon, often called the "Prince of Preachers," stands as a powerful example of someone who knew the depths of suffering and yet held fast to his faith in God. His story dismantles the myth that unwavering faith exempts us from pain or that suffering is always tied to spiritual weakness.

Spurgeon was one of the most influential Christian voices of the 19th century, preaching to thousands weekly at the Metropolitan Tabernacle in London, authoring books, and establishing ministries that are still impacting the world today. But behind his towering public ministry was a man who battled profound personal struggles.

Spurgeon endured persistent physical pain from gout, kidney disease, and other ailments. But perhaps even more deeply, he faced debilitating bouts of depression. He once described his mental anguish as "causeless depression" that was as challenging as his physical illnesses. This was not fleeting sadness but a recurring and heavy darkness that he carried throughout much of his life.

His struggles were not without reason. Spurgeon experienced great personal and public pressures. At age 22, a tragedy at a service he was preaching took the lives of seven people and injured many others when someone falsely cried "fire," causing a deadly stampede. Spurgeon was deeply traumatized by the event, describing it as something that cast a shadow over the rest of his life.

Yet Spurgeon's honesty about his struggles has become one of the most enduring aspects of his legacy. He didn't hide his pain behind a facade of cheerfulness or stoicism. Instead, he spoke openly about his challenges, even from the pulpit, showing his congregation that faith is not the absence of struggle but the decision to trust God in the midst of it.

Spurgeon's view of suffering was deeply rooted in his understanding of God's sovereignty and goodness. He didn't see his depression or physical pain as divine punishment but as part of God's refining work. He famously said, "I have learned to kiss the wave that throws me against the Rock of Ages." For Spurgeon, suffering was a means by which he drew nearer to God—a way to experience God's grace more fully. This perspective didn't come easily, nor did it negate the pain he experienced. But it allowed him to see purpose in the trial. Spurgeon's theology gave him room to cry out to God in his darkest moments while still holding onto the truth of God's goodness and love.

Spurgeon's openness about his suffering is a gift to the Church. He dismantled the myth that Christians must always be joyful or that admitting struggle is a sign of weak faith. He showed that faith can coexist with pain, doubt, and even depression. His honesty has encouraged countless Christians to be vulnerable about their own struggles, reminding us that God's power is made perfect in our weakness (2 Corinthians 12:9).

In a sermon addressing his congregation, Spurgeon said, "The mind can descend far lower than the body, for in it there are bottomless pits. The flesh can bear only a certain number of wounds and no more, but the soul can bleed in ten thousand ways, and die over and over again each hour." This raw acknowledgment of emotional and mental suffering resonates deeply, especially in a world that often struggles to connect faith with mental health.

Spurgeon continued to preach and minister to others, not because he was free of pain but because he trusted that God was faithful even in the midst of it. For those who feel overwhelmed by suffering, Spurgeon's story offers hope. It reminds us that our struggles don't disqualify us from God's love or plans. Instead, they can deepen our dependence on Him and shape our understanding of His grace.

Myth: God Won't Give You More Than You Can Handle

Ah, the infamous phrase: "God won't give you more than you can handle." It's tossed around as a balm for the overwhelmed and weary, but let's be honest—it often feels more like a band-aid slapped on a gaping wound. The problem is, this saying isn't biblical, at least not in the way people use it. It's a misinterpretation of 1 Corinthians 10:13, which says:

> *No temptation has overtaken you except what is com-*
> *mon to mankind. And God is faithful; he will not let*
> *you be tempted beyond what you can bear. But when*
> *you are tempted, he will also provide a way out so that*
> *you can endure it.*

1 Corinthians 10:13 NIV

Notice something? This verse is about temptation, not suffering. It's a promise that God will help us resist sin—not a guarantee that life will always stay within the boundaries of what we think we can handle. The truth is, life will absolutely give you more than you can handle. And sometimes, that's the point. If we could handle everything on our own, we wouldn't need God. That's not a weakness—it's by design.

Take the story of Corrie ten Boom, a Dutch Christian who, along with her family, risked everything to hide Jews from the Nazis during World War II. Eventually, Corrie and her sister Betsie were caught and sent to Ravensbrück, one of the most brutal concentration camps. The suffering they endured was unimaginable—starvation, disease, relentless cruelty, and the constant shadow of death. Betsie, frail and sick, was especially vulnerable.

At one point, Corrie found herself completely overwhelmed. She cried out to God, struggling to understand why He was allowing such evil. How could they endure this? It was too much. And it was. Corrie didn't have the strength on her own. None of us would.

But Betsie, even in her weakened state, had an unshakeable faith. She reminded Corrie, "There is no pit so deep that God's love is not deeper still." Betsie's faith wasn't rooted in the idea that God would make their suffering disappear. It was rooted in the truth that God's presence was enough to sustain them. And that's exactly what He did. Betsie eventually died in that camp, but her faith never wavered. Corrie survived and spent the rest of her life sharing their story, a testament to the God who carried them through the valley of death.

This myth about "handling it" creates a dangerous expectation. It isolates us, making us feel like failures when the weight of life is too heavy to bear. But here's the thing: acknowledging that we can't handle it isn't a sign of weakness—it's a sign of faith. It's the moment we admit that we need God and others to step in and help. And help doesn't mean we instantly feel better or that the problem is solved. It means we are not alone.

So, what do you do when life gives you more than you can handle? First, lean on God. Rest in His grace, trust His promises, and believe that He is enough. Second, don't try to carry it all alone. God designed us for community, for bearing each other's burdens (Galatians 6:2). It's okay to admit you need help. Sometimes, that help comes through a prayer that shifts our perspective or a friend who sits with us in our grief. Sometimes, it's just holding on, one day at a time, trusting that God's strength will get us through.

Finally, **let go of the idea that you have to be a superhero.**

God isn't asking you to carry it all. He's asking you to bring it to Him. And that's where the beauty of this truth comes in: life will give you more than you can handle, but it will never be more than God can handle. And He's in it with you, step by step, day by day, offering the kind of strength that only comes from His presence.

So when you hear someone say, "God won't give you more than you can handle," gently remind them: it's okay if you can't handle it, because God can. And He's right there, ready to carry you through.

Dale's Story

I grew up in church and began following Jesus at the age of nine, so it wasn't too surprising when I decided to pursue a career in ministry. At first, I thought my path was music, but over time, I felt called to pastoral ministry.

I met my wife in high school—love at first sight, at least for me. She was the love of my life. We got married while we were in college, and after that, we went to seminary so I could continue my training. But I struggled in school. Eventually, I left seminary and returned to my hometown, looking for a place to serve in ministry. In those early years, I worked in several churches, but I wrestled deeply with my calling. I battled a poor self-image and felt inadequate as a pastor.

In the early 2000s, I started a church in a suburb of my hometown. I truly believed God had called me to pastor. I loved working with people and felt confident that this was exactly what He wanted me to do.

Then, in early 2005, while I was still pastoring, Kim—my wife—began having seizures. Soon, we learned the unthinkable: she had a cancerous brain tumor.

Really? The love of my life? I had given my entire life to Christian ministry, and this is what happened? I couldn't help but think about all the people who had lived only for themselves, never giving God a second thought—why not them? Why her?

The doctor told us she had, at most, nine months to live. What followed was a year of chemo and radiation. And after that? Surgery to remove the tumor—with the terrifying risks of paralysis or even death.

I didn't handle it well. Kim was the one with faith. I was a mess. I tried to pray for her before surgery, but all I could do was blubber. She, on the other hand, was sharing with the pre-op nurses about how God was working in her life. Later, someone told me they couldn't believe how calm and trusting she was, given her circumstances. People used to tell us, "You have great faith." Maybe she did. Me? Not so much. I always told people, "I don't have great faith. I have faith in a great God."

Kim was a nurse, but after surgery, she could no longer work. She developed constant, unbearable leg pain—something the doctors couldn't diagnose. She became dependent on pain medication, yet nothing seemed to help. Pain, 24/7. Doctor after doctor, but no relief.

She was the love of my life, but suddenly, I was her caretaker. And I didn't feel like a husband anymore. I struggled with that. Over and over, I cried out, "God, why me? I gave You my life, and now this? I don't understand."

We navigated those years the best we could. Kim struggled with losing control over her own body, so she tried to control our family instead. The kids didn't understand why their mother had changed. Why she wasn't the same mom they had always known. The strain was heavy, relationships were hurt, and I did my best to mediate—to keep the peace. Some days were better than others.

As time went on, the effects of the tumor and surgery worsened. Kim began to forget things—her mother's death, our grandchildren's names. She slept all day, mixed up her days and nights, and eventually, she developed stroke-like symptoms that left her unable to use her right side. She became wheelchair-bound. Eventually, I had no choice but to place her in a nursing home where she could receive the 24-hour care she needed.

In September 2021, Kim suffered a massive hemorrhagic stroke. She never woke up. Three days later, she was gone.

I grew up with a legalistic view of God. I believed that for Him to love me, I had to be good. I had to follow the rules. When I did, He loved me. When I didn't, I felt like a failure—like He was disappointed in me.

I saw that same belief surface in my life with Kim. I kept wondering if I had done something wrong. Was I suffering for Jesus?

But listen to this—please don't miss it. My life as a believer is not about rules and regulations. It's about a relationship.

God's love for me is not based on my actions. He loves me. Period. Not because of how I act. Not because of what I do.

Now, don't misunderstand me—I can't just live however I want. You can't marry someone and then live like you're single. But at the same time, just following a set of rules doesn't make you married.

Love does.

I didn't have to take care of Kim. I chose to. Even in the hardest moments—when I struggled, when I was angry at God, and sometimes at her—it was my honor and my privilege to care for her.

No one would have faulted me if I had walked away. No one should have to do that. But that's exactly what God did for me through Jesus.

He didn't have to give His life. He chose to. He did it because He wanted to. He did it out of love. He wanted me back.

Kim loved me—and for some reason I'll never understand, she loved me first. A nerdy, nonathletic, skinny, unattractive boy. But she loved me.

Caring for her was my way of showing how blessed I was to have her. My way of saying thank you for her undeserved love. One more time: I cared for her out of love, not obligation.

As she neared the end, I lost more and more of the woman I loved. She never stopped loving me. She never stopped wanting to be with me. But as I looked into her eyes, I saw the blank stare of a disease that was slowly stealing her away.

If you are walking through something like this, I won't pretend I understand. Everyone's journey is different. But I do know this—Jesus made only one promise that never failed.

Does Jesus heal? Yes, absolutely. Did I stop praying because I didn't see it? No. I wanted my wife back, and I probably wore Jesus out asking.

Does He promise that we won't suffer if we follow Him? No. This world is broken, and we suffer its consequences. Somewhere along the way, we've done people a disservice by making them think that following Jesus means a life of ease. Jesus told us we would suffer. I think we forgot that part. But here's what He did promise me—and He never failed. He promised never to leave me or forsake me.

Through every up and down, through every cry of "This isn't fair, God!"—He never left me. He sat with me in my suffering. He shared His love for me and for Kim.

Even if God had answered my prayer—if the cost of getting my miracle meant losing Jesus—my answer would have been no.

As much as I loved Kim, as much as she was part of my life for 48 years, I need Jesus even more. My life is nothing without Him.

And if Jesus is who He says He is, then I will see Kim again. I will spend eternity with the love of my life. I often think about this: No matter what, I haven't lost.

I got to spend my life with the woman I loved. I got to raise my children, hold my grandchildren, and make memories that filled life with meaning.

That hope carries me. It reminds me that even in the deepest loss, there is still a greater promise ahead.

Please, don't let feelings, emotions, or the opinions of others determine your eternity. You don't have to earn God's love.

He already loves you.

The only thing standing between you and His love—is you. The man in the Bible who suffered the most, second only to Jesus, was Job. I love the way he put it:

> *But as for me, I know that my Redeemer lives, and He will stand upon the earth at last.*
>
> Job 19:25 NLT

CHAPTER FOUR

THE MAN OF SORROWS

From the moment Jesus entered the world, His life was marked by suffering. The prophet Isaiah foretold this reality centuries before His birth:

> *He was despised and rejected by men, a man of sorrows, and acquainted with grief.*
>
> Isaiah 53:3 NIV

What a way to describe a coming Messiah! The long-awaited Savior, the one prophesied to crush the serpent's head and establish a kingdom without end, is portrayed not in terms of power or grandeur but as a figure of sorrow and suffering. Isaiah's prophecy doesn't paint the Messiah as a warrior draped in glory or a king sitting on a throne of gold. Instead, it describes Him as "a man of sorrows, acquainted with grief" (Isaiah 53:3).

This description seems almost upside down compared

to what we might expect. A deliverer should exude strength, triumph, and victory, right? Someone to rally behind with shouts of celebration and songs of conquest. But here, we're told the Messiah will be despised and rejected, bearing the burdens of a broken world. It's not a triumphant rallying cry; it's a sobering reminder of the cost of redemption.

Imagine hearing those words centuries before Jesus came, longing for liberation from oppression. What hope would a "man of sorrows" offer? Yet, this prophecy is God's way of turning our expectations on their heads. The Messiah wouldn't deliver through dominance but through sacrifice. He wouldn't avoid pain but embrace it, taking it on Himself for the sake of the world.

In those few words, "a man of sorrows," we see the depth of God's plan. It's a Messiah who understands our suffering because He shares in it. It's a Savior who doesn't just look down on our pain from a distance but enters into it, walking with us through it.

Royalty In Rags

Jesus didn't step into humanity cloaked in immunity; He entered it fully exposed to its raw and aching realities. He came vulnerable, embracing the full spectrum of human pain and sorrow from the moment He drew His first breath.

Consider the circumstances of His birth: the King of kings didn't arrive in a majestic palace surrounded by luxury and grandeur. Instead, He was born in the humblest of settings—a stable. He wasn't exactly greeted with fanfare either. There wasn't even room for Him at the inn or anywhere else in Bethlehem. He got the scraps of hospitality—a borrowed space in the back, where animals usually stayed.

The reality of His entry into the world was gritty and harsh. He didn't arrive to the comfort of silk sheets or royal fanfare but to the earthy smell of animals and the coarse straw of a feeding trough. The cold night air would have hit His newborn skin, and like any other baby, He likely cried—His tiny lungs filling with the chill of a world that was far from welcoming.

Mary and Joseph, weary from their journey, wrapped Him in swaddling cloths and laid Him in that makeshift crib, a manger meant to hold feed for livestock. The scene wasn't picturesque or serene—it was striking in its humility. The Savior of the world, the One through whom all things were made, was cradled in a trough, in a place no parent would choose for their child. It wasn't posh; it was pathetic. And yet, it was profoundly purposeful.

This is how God chose to enter our brokenness—not above it, but right in the middle of it. From His very first moments, Jesus' life whispered a truth that would echo through His ministry: He was not distant from our pain. He came to share it, to feel it, and ultimately to redeem it.

Jesus The Refugee

Shortly after His birth, Jesus' family fled to Egypt to escape the horrors of King Herod's massacre of infants—a tragedy we know as the Slaughter of the Innocents (Matthew 2:13-18). This event, foretold by the prophet Jeremiah, fulfilled the chilling words:

> *A voice is heard in Ramah, weeping and great mourning, Rachel weeping for her children and refusing to be comforted, because they are no more.*

Matthew 2:18 (referencing Jeremiah 31:15)

The danger to Jesus' life was immediate and real. An angel of the Lord appeared to Joseph in a dream, warning him: "Get up, take the child and his mother and escape to Egypt. Stay there until I tell you, for Herod is going to search for the child to kill him" (Matthew 2:13). Imagine the scene as Mary and Joseph, still adjusting to the reality of being parents, awoke in the dead of night to make their escape. They packed in haste, likely taking only what they could carry, and began the long, uncertain journey to Egypt with their newborn son.

The journey itself must have been grueling. Mary, still recovering from childbirth, and Joseph, burdened with the responsibility of protecting his family, traveled through harsh terrain to reach an entirely unfamiliar land. The echoes of Herod's cruelty—the cries of grieving mothers and fathers in Bethlehem—would have been fresh in their minds, amplifying the urgency of their flight.

For Jesus, the Son of God, to begin His earthly life as a refugee is a profound testament to the depth of His identification with humanity. This early displacement foreshadowed His life—a life of rejection, opposition, and hardship. Even as a baby, He was surrounded by a fallen world's dangers and harsh realities.

This moment in the story also reminds us that God's plans often unfold amid chaos and pain. The journey to

Egypt was not an accident or an oversight—it was part of the divine plan to protect the Messiah and fulfill the prophecies about Him. The same God who orchestrated this escape would continue to guide Jesus' path, even when that path led to the ultimate suffering of the cross.

Divine Frailty

One of the most profound mysteries of the Christian faith is the dual nature of Christ: that Jesus was both fully God and fully man. This union, known as the hypostatic union, is central to understanding who Jesus is and how He lived among us. The doctrine of the hypostatic union teaches that Jesus Christ is fully God and fully human, united in one person without division or confusion.

A helpful illustration is to think of a coin with two sides—heads and tails. Each side is distinct, yet they are inseparably part of the same coin. In the same way, Jesus possesses two distinct natures, divine and human, perfectly united in His person. While this analogy cannot fully capture the mystery, it offers a glimpse into one of the most beautiful truths of our faith. In Jesus, we see the infinite God taking on human frailty—not just appearing human but fully entering into the limitations and vulnerabilities of our existence.

The apostle Paul describes this divine humility in Philippians 2:6-8 (NIV):

> *Who, being in very nature God, did not consider equality with God something to be used to his own advantage; rather, he made himself nothing by taking*

> *the very nature of a servant, being made in human*
> *likeness. And being found in appearance as a man,*
> *he humbled himself by becoming obedient to death—*
> *even death on a cross!*

Jesus, though eternally God, willingly set aside His divine privileges to take on humanity. This wasn't a temporary disguise or a shedding of His divinity; He remained fully God while fully embracing the reality of being human. In the words of the early church fathers, He was "perfect in Godhead and also perfect in manhood; truly God and truly man."

Jesus wasn't just pretending to experience these things; He fully entered into them. For example:

Hunger: In the wilderness, Satan tempted Jesus to turn stones into bread, exploiting His physical hunger (Matthew 4:3). Yet Jesus relied on God's Word, showing us how to trust God even in our weakness.

Fatigue: After a full day of teaching and healing, Jesus fell asleep on a boat, so exhausted that even a storm couldn't wake Him until His disciples panicked (Mark 4:38). His need for rest reminds us that He was not immune to the demands of a physical body.

Limited Time: Despite being God, Jesus didn't heal every person or preach in every town during His earthly ministry. He prioritized prayer and obedience to the Father's will, showing us that human limitations don't diminish our ability to fulfill God's purposes.

Emotional Pain: Jesus wept at the tomb of Lazarus (John 11:35). He grieved over Jerusalem's rejection of Him

(Luke 13:34). In Gethsemane, He experienced anguish so intense that He sweat drops of blood (Luke 22:44). These moments reveal a Savior who fully understands the depth of human sorrow.

Physical Pain: It goes without saying that Jesus wasn't immune to physical pain and even trauma. The physical pain Jesus endured during His crucifixion was excruciating, and it provides a profound glimpse into the suffering He willingly underwent for humanity.

Acquainted With Grief

Jesus not only experienced suffering; He was deeply acquainted with it. His life was a journey through sorrow, culminating in the ultimate suffering on the cross. The Gospels provide a vivid picture of a Savior who carried grief—not only His own but the grief of the world.

One of the most poignant moments in Jesus' ministry is also the shortest verse in Scripture (John 11:35):

Jesus wept.

Standing at the tomb of His friend Lazarus, Jesus was overwhelmed by the sorrow of death and the pain it inflicted on those He loved. Picture the scene: Martha, her voice breaking with despair, says, "Lord, if you had been here, my brother would not have died" (John 11:21). Mary falls at His feet, her tears soaking the ground. The crowd of mourners wails, their grief palpable. And in the midst of it all, Jesus stands—the Son of God, who holds the power of life and death—and He weeps.

Why would Jesus weep when He knew He was about to

raise Lazarus from the dead? In *The Prophetic Imagination*, Walter Brueggemann reflects on the significance of Jesus' tears: "Weeping must be real because endings are real… Suffering made audible and visible produces hope; articulated grief is the gate of newness." Jesus' weeping was not just an emotional response. It was a profound acknowledgment of the brokenness of the world and the deep cost of love. He felt the sting of death—its ability to fracture relationships, devastate families, and fill the world with sorrow.

But Jesus didn't stop at weeping. Imagine the tension as He approaches the tomb. The stone is rolled away, the smell of decay wafting into the air. The crowd murmurs their doubts. And then, with a loud voice, Jesus calls, "Lazarus, come out!" (John 11:43). The impossible happens: Lazarus emerges, bound in grave clothes, a living testimony to the power of God over death. This moment gives us a glimpse of Jesus' ultimate mission—not just to comfort us in sorrow but to defeat the very source of it.

Despised And Rejected

Jesus' path to the cross was not only marked by physical suffering but also by the devastating emotional pain of betrayal and rejection. These wounds cut deep, striking at His relationships and laying bare human loyalty's fragile, fickle nature. If you've ever been betrayed or abandoned by someone you trusted, you can take comfort in knowing that Jesus understands this pain intimately.

Betrayal by a Friend: Judas Iscariot, one of the twelve disciples, is the most infamous betrayer in history. Judas walked with Jesus for three years, heard His teaching, witnessed His miracles, and shared meals with Him. Yet, despite this close relationship, Judas would betray Jesus for only thirty pieces of silver (Matthew 26:14-16).

In the Garden of Gethsemane, knowing the suffering that awaited Him, He fell to the ground and prayed, "My soul is very sorrowful, even to death" (Matthew 26:38). Luke tells us that His anguish was so intense that His sweat became like drops of blood falling to the ground (Luke 22:44). The disciples, unable to grasp the depth of His sorrow, fell asleep. Yet even in His anguish, Jesus submitted to the Father's will, saying, "Not as I will, but as you will" (Matthew 26:39).

And just moments later, in that garden, Judas would arrive with a mob armed with swords and clubs, leading them to the very place where Jesus was praying. His signal? A kiss—an intimate gesture twisted into an act of treachery (Matthew 26:48-50). Imagine the heartbreak as Judas approached. Jesus, fully aware of what was about to happen, still addressed him as "friend." The weight of this moment reveals Jesus' compassion, even in the face of betrayal.

Abandonment by Friends: The betrayal of Judas was only the beginning. As Jesus was arrested and led away, the rest of His disciples scattered in fear (Mark 14:50). These were the men who had sworn loyalty to Him, who had witnessed His glory on the Mount of Transfiguration and declared their willingness to die for Him (Matthew 26:35). Yet, in His hour of greatest need, they abandoned Him.

Perhaps the most poignant of these betrayals was Peter's denial. Just hours after boldly proclaiming that he would never forsake Jesus, Peter denied even knowing Him—not once, but three times (Luke 22:54-62). When the rooster crowed, fulfilling Jesus' earlier prediction, Peter realized the gravity of his actions and wept bitterly. For Jesus, this moment must have been crushing. The one He called the "rock" (Matthew 16:18) had crumbled under pressure.

Rejection by the Crowds: Beyond the betrayal of His friends, Jesus endured the rejection of the very people He came to save. The crowds that once shouted "Hosanna!" as He entered Jerusalem (Matthew 21:9) now cried out, "Crucify Him!" (Mark 15:13-14). The religious leaders, who should have recognized Him as the promised Messiah, plotted His death. Even as He hung on the cross, passersby mocked Him, hurling insults and taunting Him to save Himself (Matthew 27:39-43).

This rejection was foretold by the prophet Isaiah: "He was despised and rejected by men, a man of sorrows and acquainted with grief" (Isaiah 53:3). Jesus didn't just face isolated acts of betrayal; He bore the collective rejection of humanity, embodying the sorrow of a world that turned its back on its Savior.

What's remarkable about Jesus' suffering is how He responded. He didn't retaliate or harden His heart. Instead, He forgave. As He hung on the cross, with the echoes of mockery still ringing in His ears, Jesus prayed, "Father, forgive them, for they know not what they do" (Luke 23:34). This radical forgiveness reveals the depth of His love and the purpose of His mission: to reconcile a broken and rebellious humanity to God.

If you've ever experienced betrayal or rejection, you are not alone. Jesus understands. He felt the sting of betrayal from a friend's kiss, the ache of abandonment by those He loved, and the agony of rejection by the very people He came to save. His experience offers profound comfort: He walks with you in your pain, knowing it firsthand.

But His suffering also challenges us. Jesus' response to betrayal and rejection calls us to a higher way—a way of forgiveness, grace, and steadfast love. It reminds us that while human relationships may fail, God's love never does. As the psalmist writes, "Though my father and mother forsake me, the Lord will receive me" (Psalm 27:10). In the face of betrayal and rejection, Jesus remained faithful, showing us the power of love to overcome even the deepest wounds.

A Criminal's Treatment

As the final hours of Jesus' life began, He faced the full weight of human cruelty and divine purpose. Betrayed by a friend, abandoned by His followers, and handed over to those who mocked and beat Him, the stage was set for the most excruciating ordeal imaginable. What followed was the culmination of a life marked by suffering, leading to the cross where love and sacrifice would meet in the ultimate act of redemption.

In *Dominion: How the Christian Revolution Remade the World*, Tom Holland reflects on the profound significance of the crucifixion: "That a man who had himself been crucified might be hailed as a god could not help but be seen by people everywhere across the Roman world as scandalous, obscene, grotesque." It was this very perception that led Jesus to be treated with such contempt and rejection.

Combining biblical descriptions and medical insights, we can better understand the depth of the agony of Jesus in his sacrifice:

The Scourging: Before Jesus was crucified, He was subjected to flogging, a brutal punishment that left victims on the brink of death. The Gospels record, "Then Pilate took Jesus and had him flogged" (John 19:1). Roman scourging involved the use of a *flagrum* or *cat-o'-nine-tails*—a whip with leather cords embedded with sharp pieces of bone or metal.

Medical experts describe how such a tool would rip into the skin and muscle and expose underlying tissues. Dr. C. Truman Davis, in his medical analysis of the crucifixion, notes that the lacerations would cause significant blood loss and immense pain, leaving the body weakened and in shock. Isaiah's prophecy about the Messiah reflects this suffering: "By his wounds we are healed" (Isaiah 53:5).

The Crown of Thorns: After the scourging, Roman soldiers mocked Jesus by pressing a crown of thorns onto His head. Matthew records, "They twisted together a crown of thorns and set it on his head" (Matthew 27:29). This wasn't just symbolic humiliation. The scalp is one of the most vascular areas of the body, and the sharp thorns likely pierced deeply, causing profuse bleeding and adding to the physical torment. The mockery magnified His emotional and physical suffering, fulfilling the prophecy that He would be "despised and rejected" (Isaiah 53:3).

Carrying the Cross: Following the flogging and crowning, Jesus was forced to carry His own crossbeam to

Golgotha (John 19:17). The *patibulum*, or horizontal beam of the cross, could weigh 75–125 pounds. After the intense blood loss and physical trauma of the scourging, Jesus likely suffered hypovolemic shock—a state caused by extreme blood loss leading to faintness and weakness.

Luke notes that Simon of Cyrene was compelled to carry the cross for Jesus after He collapsed under its weight (Luke 23:26). This detail underscores how weakened His body had become by this point.

The Crucifixion: Crucifixion was designed to inflict maximum pain while prolonging death. Roman soldiers nailed Jesus to the cross, likely driving 5–7-inch iron spikes through His wrists (considered part of the hand in the ancient world) and feet (Luke 24:39-40).

Medical experts explain that the nails would sever major nerves in the wrists, causing excruciating, radiating pain known as causalgia. His feet, nailed together, bore the strain of supporting His body weight. Every breath required Him to push up on His nailed feet, scraping His back—already shredded from the scourging—against the rough wood of the cross.

Psalm 22:16 prophetically speaks of this: "They pierce my hands and my feet." Jesus likely suffered from cramps, suffocation, and fluid buildup in His lungs (a condition known as pleural effusion). John 19:34 describes how, when a soldier pierced His side, blood and water flowed out—evidence of heart failure due to asphyxiation or cardiac rupture.

Beyond the physical torment, Jesus bore emotional and spiritual agony. He cried out, "My God, my God, why have you forsaken me?" (Matthew 27:46), revealing the weight of sin and separation from the Father that He carried on behalf of humanity. Isaiah foretold this spiritual anguish: "The Lord has laid on him the iniquity of us all" (Isaiah 53:6).

After hours of unimaginable pain, Jesus uttered, "It is finished," and breathed His last (John 19:30). His death was not merely the result of physical trauma; it was the culmination of bearing humanity's sin. The Gospels emphasize that His life was not taken from Him but willingly given (John 10:18).

What A Savior

Jesus' physical suffering was unparalleled, yet He endured it with a purpose: to redeem humanity. His pain reminds us of the cost of sin and the depth of God's love. As Hebrews 12:2 reminds us, "For the joy set before him he endured the cross, scorning its shame."

When He wept, it wasn't for show. When He bled, it wasn't symbolic. When He groaned in agony, it was the very real pain of a body subjected to suffering. The same Creator who spoke the universe into existence took on the limitations of a human frame.

This "divine frailty" isn't a flaw or a weakness—it's a profound expression of God's love. Jesus could have come as a conquering king, untouchable and immune to the struggles of humanity. But instead, He came as a servant, embracing our brokenness so that He might redeem it.

The writer of Hebrews captures the heart of this truth:

For we do not have a high priest who is unable to empathize with our weaknesses, but we have one who has been tempted in every way, just as we are—yet he did not sin.

Hebrews 4:15 NIV

Immanuel

C.S. Lewis wrote in *A Grief Observed*, "Pain insists upon being attended to. God whispers to us in our pleasures, speaks in our conscience, but shouts in our pains: it is His megaphone to rouse a deaf world." On the cross, Jesus shouted a message of love, redemption, and solidarity with humanity. His suffering assures us that God is not distant or indifferent but deeply present in our pain.

The cross itself is the ultimate demonstration of Jesus walking through suffering. On Calvary, He bore the full weight of humanity's sin and sorrow. His death was not the end but the beginning of redemption. The resurrection transformed the cross from a symbol of death into a symbol of hope, reminding us that our suffering is not the final word.

As we face trials, we can rest in the truth that Jesus is with us, that He understands our pain, and that He will walk us through it. And as we follow Him, we can trust that He will bring beauty from ashes and joy from mourning, just as He promised. Through His suffering, we find hope—and through our suffering, we share in His glory. Henri Nouwen captures this beautifully in *The Wounded Healer*: "The way of the cross is not a way of despair, but of hope, for it leads to resurrection."

It's a good time to pause and pray, reflecting on Jesus' sacrifice and presence in the midst of your own suffering:

> *Jesus,*
> *Thank You for loving me so much that You endured pain and suffering for my sake. Thank You for the cross and for making a way for me to be forgiven and close to You. When life feels overwhelming, remind me that You understand my pain because You've experienced it too. Thank You for being with me in every moment, bringing comfort and hope even in the hardest times.*
> *I trust You, Jesus, and I'm so grateful for Your love.*
> *Amen.*

Daisy's Story

If you saw me on the street, you'd see a girl smiling, seemingly carefree. But if you sat down and shared a meal with me, you'd hear the rich layers of truth behind that smile. It's not that I lack worries, grievances, or loss. I smile because life's pain has drawn me closer to God, producing a deep well of gratefulness and joy.

I am a mother of three beautiful children, each uniquely made. They have brought immeasurable joy into my life but also unexpected challenges. Two of my children face disabilities that place limits on their lives, while their older sibling has had to navigate this journey alongside them. Each of them has specific needs, and I learned early on that my own wisdom and strength would never be enough. Only God could sustain me. I knew I needed Him.

As their mother, I have always wanted the best for them. But the truth is, that's not always what they've gotten from me.

There was a time when I was in a place of deep discouragement, weighed down by unanswered prayers for my family's healing. I was constantly disappointed by medical results and overwhelmed by the sheer volume of paperwork and problems that filled my days. My natural response—my kryptonite—was to shove those emotions under the rug, convincing myself that everything was fine, even when I could hardly keep my head above water. As if that wasn't enough, I placed immense pressure on myself as a single mom, believing I had to solve everything on my own to prove that I was doing a good job.

But here was the truth: I publicly professed my trust in Jesus, yet the reality of my life often contradicted those words. I was running on empty. Once pure-hearted, I had become hardened and weary, trapped in survival mode, void of any real peace.

Today, I live a different truth. The challenges that fill my plate remain, but the key difference is that I have surrendered them to Jesus. I no longer pour from an empty cup.

It wasn't an overnight change—it took years.

Healing needed to happen. Hard emotions needed to be pulled out from under the rug. I had to understand that God loves my children more than I can imagine and that He walks with them just as He walks with me. Even in my brokenness, He never left my side.

It all began with honest conversations with God. I

came to understand that grieving the losses my children and I have faced was essential for my healing. I had to accept that normalcy was not in the cards for us and that society's limitations on my children might restrict opportunities. Yet, faith revealed its beauty—it provided God a platform to showcase His presence. And He has done this time and time again.

Through this grieving process, He reminded me of the reasons behind my smile. Sometimes, all it takes is unarchiving the miracles of the past to see Heaven on Earth once again.

Twelve years ago, my daughter couldn't speak. After countless meetings with specialists and therapies, I often left feeling discouraged and unresourced. But I refused to give up. As her voice, I fought to ensure she had what she needed. Today, she has a gift of unfiltered gab and a surprising talent for math that she pulls out as a party trick.

Eleven years ago, my sweet boy entered the world. Just ten hours after his birth, doctors delivered gut-wrenching news—he would likely endure lifelong seizures and spasms. The fear and uncertainty hit me like a weight in my chest. Yet, miraculously, by the time he was six months old, the seizures stopped.

Since then, we've navigated countless challenges—medications, paperwork, medical equipment, and mounting bills. There were moments of overwhelming stress and worry, times when I felt completely lost. Yet through it all, God has supernaturally provided in ways I never could have imagined.

Eighteen years ago, God had their big brother in mind

before his two siblings were even born. His character has been beautifully refined through every challenge we've faced together. In moments of chaos, his calmness is a guiding light. His love for his younger siblings is unmatched—gentle, patient, and always present. Watching him grow into the compassionate and empathetic young man he is today has been one of my greatest joys.

Five years ago, I found myself learning how to carry a burden meant for two people. It was overwhelming, filled with moments of doubt and struggle. Yet, in that heaviness, God surrounded us with a community that lifted us when we needed it most. They reminded me that I wasn't alone. I carried the image of Christ more by leaning on my community than I ever did by trying to figure it all out alone.

The fruit is evident.

Joy—in witnessing all the victories, because even the smallest ones are miracles to us.

Love—from the unwavering support of our community, whose gentleness and compassion have carried us through our hardest moments.

Peace—the kind that has enveloped me in hospital rooms, in moments of silent desperation, on solitary walks under the stars. Each time, God met me there, reminding me that I was never alone.

Through it all, I know my children have watched me closely. I pray that my words have consistently reflected my actions. I know I've had moments where I've fallen short, but I hope they see how God has carried me through. I pray they understand that even in our struggles, there is purpose. We have learned resilience. We have learned gratitude. We have learned to persevere. Each obstacle has not only deepened our faith but has strengthened our bond as a family and our connection to a loving, faithful God.

Life's trials are inevitable, and I know there will still be moments when I feel overwhelmed. But I am confident of this: God's fingerprints are all over my life, reminding me that He has always been there. And He always will be.

> *Consider it pure joy, my brothers and sisters, whenever you face trials of many kinds, because you know that the testing of your faith produces perseverance.*
>
> James 1:2-3

> *He has made everything beautiful in its time.*
>
> Ecclesiastes 3:11

> *The Lord himself goes before you and will be with you; he will never leave you nor forsake you.*
>
> Deuteronomy 31:8

> *For I know the plans I have for you," declares the Lord, "plans to prosper you and not to harm you, plans to give you hope and a future.*
>
> Jeremiah 29:11

CHAPTER FIVE

THE LONG SHADOW OF LOSS

How do you put grief into words? Defining it feels almost impossible because it's intensely personal and deeply felt. Every explanation falls short of capturing the raw reality of actually living through it. But we try anyway, don't we? We fumble for words to describe something that defies neat categories, something that's more a storm than a season, more a journey than a destination. Grief is the ache of love unfulfilled, the weight of absence, the silent reshaping of a life that will never quite look the same. It's a universal experience, yet profoundly individual—no two people walk through it the same way, and no one comes out untouched.

Grief is our natural response to loss. When most people hear the word, they immediately think of mourning the death of a loved one—and, of course, that's one of its deepest and most universal expressions. But grief isn't confined to funerals, memorials, or the passing of someone dear. It's a much broader experience woven into the fabric of human existence. Grief touches every part of life where loss is felt.

Grief can be about the obvious things—like the death of a parent, spouse, or child—but it also surfaces in less recognized places. You might grieve the end of a close friendship, a broken engagement, or the betrayal of someone you trusted.

But it doesn't stop there. Grief often comes in subtler, quieter forms. You can grieve a dream that never materialized or the loss of expectations you held so tightly for years. Grief can creep in when your health takes a turn, when a long-prayed-for career goal goes unfulfilled, or when you realize that the life you imagined isn't the life you're living.

This "wider" grief, as one might call it, is less obvious but just as profound. Psychologists have long recognized the impact of these intangible losses. Pauline Boss, a researcher and author, describes this as "ambiguous loss," a kind of mourning without clear resolution. It's the ache of something undefined—the loss of what could have been. You grieve the family dynamic you always hoped for, the child you might never have, or the version of yourself you wish you could be. These losses are often invisible to the outside world, yet they are no less real.

Scripture doesn't shy away from the breadth of grief. The Psalms are filled with cries of anguish, many of which come from unmet longings or shattered dreams. Psalm 42:3 says, "My tears have been my food day and night, while people say to me all day long, 'Where is your God?'" These verses capture the essence of sorrow that goes beyond physical death—they speak to the pain of feeling abandoned, disillusioned, or broken by life's unrelenting disappointments.

Grief, whether loud and visible or quiet and hidden, is deeply personal and utterly unique. C.S. Lewis, reflecting on his own mourning in A Grief Observed, wrote, "No one ever told me that grief felt so like fear. I am not afraid, but the sensation is like being afraid." Grief is a tangled web of emotions—sadness, anger, confusion, and sometimes numbness—that ebbs and flows, often surprising us with its intensity.

We tend to view grief as a linear process, expecting that, with enough time, we'll move past it and "heal." But that's not how grief works. It doesn't follow a straight path or adhere to a timeline.

Elisabeth Kübler-Ross's five stages of grief—denial, anger, bargaining, depression, and acceptance—offer a framework to help us understand the emotional journey that often accompanies loss. While these stages don't always come in order, and not everyone experiences all of them, they give us language to describe what we're feeling and why.

Denial: *"This Can't Be Happening."* Denial is often our mind's first line of defense against overwhelming pain. It's the shock absorber that keeps the full weight of grief from crushing us all at once. You might find yourself thinking, This isn't real. This can't be happening. Denial isn't about rejecting reality—it's about giving your heart time to catch up to what your mind already knows. It's a natural and necessary first step, allowing us to begin processing the unthinkable.

Anger: *"Why Is This Happening?"* Anger can feel like an unwelcome guest, but it's a valid part of grief. You might feel angry at the circumstances, the person you've lost, or even God. Why did this happen? Why now? Anger is often rooted in the pain of injustice or the helplessness of loss. It can feel like a raging storm inside, but it's important to let it out in healthy ways. God is big enough to handle your anger, and bringing it to Him is okay. In fact, the psalms are full of examples of raw, honest frustration poured out before God.

Bargaining: *"If Only…"* Bargaining is the stage where we start playing the if only game. If only I had done this differently.If only they had gotten help sooner. It's an attempt to regain some sense of control in a situation where control has been taken away. Bargaining can also take the form of promises to God: If You fix this, I'll do anything. It's our way of wrestling with the reality of loss while still holding on to a thread of hope that things might somehow turn out differently.

Depression: *"This Is So Heavy."* When the reality of loss sinks in, it can feel like an unbearable weight. This stage is marked by profound sadness, loneliness, and a sense of despair. You might feel like the world has lost its color or like nothing will ever feel normal again. Depression is not a sign of weakness or a lack of faith—it's a natural response to significant loss. In this stage, we often come face-to-face with the depth of our pain. Even here,

God meets us.

Acceptance: *"This Is My Reality Now."* Acceptance isn't about being okay with what happened or pretending the pain is gone. It's about acknowledging the new reality and beginning to adapt to it. You might think I still hurt, but I'm starting to see a way forward. Acceptance doesn't mean you stop grieving; it means you learn to live alongside your grief. It's where healing begins—not because the pain is gone, but because you've learned how to carry it.

Again, these stages were never meant to be rigid or sequential. Grief is as unique as the person experiencing it. Grief is also cyclical. It can lie dormant for weeks, months, or even years, resurfacing when we least expect it. A song on the radio, a family tradition, a holiday, or an anniversary can bring it all rushing back. That's why it's so important to acknowledge the broader scope of grief. When we fail to name and recognize it, we risk bottling it up, only for it to spill out in other ways—through anxiety, bitterness, or even physical illness.

As believers, we have the privilege of bringing our grief to the foot of the cross, where Jesus Himself endured the ultimate loss. Jesus knew grief intimately, not only in His own suffering but in carrying the weight of the world's pain. Because He bore our sorrows, we can approach Him with the assurance that He understands our struggles.

Acknowledging grief in all its forms—whether it's the death of a loved one, the loss of a dream, or the breaking of a heart—isn't a sign of weakness. It's a testament to the depth of love and longing God has placed within us. Grief hurts because it matters. It's part of the human story, but more importantly, it's part of the redemptive story God is writing in us. While we grieve, we do not grieve without hope (1 Thessalonians 4:13).

So, whatever form your grief takes, know this: it is valid. It is seen. And it is an invitation to bring your pain to the One who promises to redeem it.

Grief Woven In

Throughout the grand narrative of Scripture, grief is not a footnote or a side story—it is an integral part of the fabric. From the earliest chapters of Genesis to the final pages of Revelation, we see grief unfold in countless lives, often in ways that feel deeply familiar to our own experiences. The Bible doesn't shy away from sorrow; instead, it confronts it head-on, inviting us to see how God meets His people in the depths of their pain.

Grief is there in the anguished cries of the psalmists, in the lamentations of the prophets, and in the heartfelt prayers of individuals like Hannah, Job, and David. It appears in the mourning of entire nations and in the quiet tears of a single soul. These stories are not distant or sterile; they are raw, human, and deeply relatable. They remind us that sorrow is not foreign to faith—it's part of the journey.

The story of David and Jonathan's friendship is one of the most profound examples of deep human connection found in Scripture. Their relationship was marked by loyalty, covenantal love, and mutual respect—a bond that transcended family ties and political allegiances. When

Jonathan died in battle alongside his father, King Saul, David was overcome with grief. His lament, recorded in 2 Samuel 1:17-27, provides a poignant window into his sorrow and the profound loss he felt.

The Loss Of A Friend

Imagine the scene: David, the warrior-king, waiting anxiously for news from the battlefield. His heart is heavy with concern—not just for his men but his dearest friend, Jonathan. Then, a messenger arrives, his face ashen, his clothes torn, and dust clinging to his hair—a sign of calamity. The words come tumbling out: "Saul and Jonathan are…dead." David's world crumbles. Grief grips him, not just for the king who pursued him but for Jonathan, the friend who stood by him through every trial. In that instant, David feels the weight of unbearable loss—a void that no victory could ever fill.

David and Jonathan's relationship was unique. The Bible describes how, from the moment they met, "Jonathan became one in spirit with David, and he loved him as himself" (1 Samuel 18:1 NIV). Despite the tension between David and Saul, Jonathan remained steadfastly loyal to David, even risking his life to protect him (1 Samuel 20:30-34). Their bond was not only a friendship but a covenantal relationship rooted in mutual trust and devotion to God.

When David learned of Jonathan's death in battle, his grief was overwhelming. David poured out his heart in raw, poetic expression in his lament, known as the *Song of the Bow*. "How the mighty have fallen!" he cried, a refrain repeated three times in the passage (2 Samuel 1:19, 25, 27 NIV). His words capture the magnitude of his loss and his deep respect for both Jonathan and Saul despite Saul's enmity toward him.

David's lament over Jonathan is more than a historical record; it's a model of grieving deeply and honestly before God and others. In 2 Samuel 1:26, David expresses his love for Jonathan with striking vulnerability: "I grieve for you, Jonathan my brother; you were very dear to me. Your love for me was wonderful, more wonderful than that of women." This verse is often misunderstood or misinterpreted, but it highlights the profound bond between these two men—a love rooted in friendship, loyalty, and covenant faithfulness.

David's lament also shows his willingness to embrace grief fully. He didn't suppress his sorrow or attempt to minimize it. Instead, he gave it voice, allowing the weight of his loss to be expressed in words and song. This willingness to lament is consistent with the biblical pattern of grieving found throughout the Psalms, where David himself often cried out to God in moments of despair. His lament demonstrates that grief and faith are not mutually exclusive. He grieved deeply, but his sorrow was held within the framework of his relationship with God. David's lament was an act of worship.

Barren And Bargaining

Hannah sat outside the temple, her heart heavy with sorrow. The sound of families celebrating nearby only deepened the ache in her soul. Her husband's other wife,

Peninnah, had once again spent the journey to Shiloh mocking her for her barrenness, each cutting word driving Hannah further into despair. She could feel the weight of her husband's love, well-meaning but insufficient to heal the longing that consumed her. The longing for a child. A son. A hope that seemed forever out of reach.

As she entered the temple, her steps were slow, and her shoulders bowed under the weight of years of unanswered prayers and unspoken shame. She knelt, trembling, tears spilling freely as she poured her anguish out to God. This was no rehearsed prayer; it was raw, desperate, and deeply vulnerable. Her lips moved silently as she begged God to see her, remember her, and answer her heart's cry. It was the prayer of a woman who had nothing left to give but her grief.

Hannah's grief wasn't just about personal longing; it carried the weight of societal judgment. Barrenness was often viewed as a divine curse or punishment in her time. Imagine the whispers as she passed through the village or joined her family on the annual pilgrimage to Shiloh to worship. Despite Elkanah's well-meaning attempts to comfort her, even declaring his love to be "better than ten sons" (1 Samuel 1:8), nothing could soothe the ache in her soul.

Within earshot of Eli, the priest, she poured out her heart before God. The text describes her praying "in deep anguish, weeping bitterly" (1 Samuel 1:10). She made a vow, promising that if God gave her a son, she would dedicate him to the Lord's service for all his days. Her prayer was raw, honest, and unfiltered—a true lament.

Eli initially misunderstood her distress, accusing her of being drunk because of the intensity of her silent cries (1 Samuel 1:12-14). But when she explained her deep sorrow, Eli blessed her, saying, "Go in peace, and may the God of Israel grant you what you have asked of him" (1 Samuel 1:17).

Hannah's response is striking. Though she didn't yet have her answer, Scripture tells us that she left the temple with her face no longer downcast (1 Samuel 1:18). Her circumstances hadn't changed, but her spirit had found solace in the act of laying her grief before God.

In time, God answered Hannah's prayer, and she gave birth to a son, Samuel, who would become one of Israel's greatest prophets. True to her vow, Hannah dedicated him to the Lord, releasing him to serve in the temple under Eli's guidance. Yet even after giving him back to God, she lifted a song of praise that reveals the depth of her faith: "My heart rejoices in the Lord; in the Lord, my horn is lifted high" (1 Samuel 2:1).

Grief can be a sacred space where we encounter God in profound ways. Hannah's willingness to bring her sorrow to the temple, to cry out in vulnerability and faith, and to trust God with her deepest longings offers us a model for grieving well. Her lament reminds us that it's okay to weep, plead, and wrestle with our pain before God. And her faith-filled response—leaving her burdens in God's hands—invites us to trust that even when the answers don't come immediately, God is still present, still listening, and still working.

A Lonely Prophet

The mighty prophet Elijah had just come off the spiritual high of a lifetime. On Mount Carmel, he had confronted the prophets of Baal in a fiery display of God's power. He stood boldly, mocking their futile cries to a powerless idol and calling down fire from heaven to consume his water-soaked offering (1 Kings 18:20-39). Victory was undeniable, and Elijah must have felt the swell of divine purpose coursing through his veins. But it didn't last.

Queen Jezebel, furious over the defeat and execution of the Baal prophets, vowed to take Elijah's life. Word of her threat reached him quickly, and the bold prophet who had just stood against hundreds now fled for his life. He ran into the wilderness, alone and afraid, his confidence shattered. Finally, beneath the shade of a broom bush, Elijah collapsed. Overwhelmed by fear, exhaustion, and a creeping sense of failure, he cried out to God: "I have had enough, Lord," he said. "Take my life; I am no better than my ancestors" (1 Kings 19:4, NIV).

Can you feel the weight of his despair? This man had seen God's power firsthand, yet now he felt completely alone, utterly defeated. The wilderness wasn't just a physical place for Elijah; it mirrored the desolation in his soul. His words echo the cry of someone who feels they have nothing left to give, no fight left in them. "I have had enough" is a universal plea for relief when the pain seems unbearable.

Elijah's grief was multi-faceted. He wasn't just afraid for his life—he felt isolated, like he was the last person left who truly followed God: "I have been very zealous for the Lord God Almighty," he lamented. "The Israelites have rejected your covenant, torn down your altars, and put your prophets to death with the sword. I am the only one left, and now they are trying to kill me too" (1 Kings 19:10, NIV). His sorrow wasn't just personal; it was tied to the perceived failure of his mission and the spiritual state of his people. Elijah was a prophet, a leader, someone who bore the weight of God's calling—and in this moment, it crushed him. He was grieving.

Yet even in Elijah's grief, God met him tenderly. First, He addressed Elijah's physical needs, providing food and water through an angel. "Get up and eat," the angel said, "for the journey is too much for you" (1 Kings 19:7, NIV). This simple act reminds us that sometimes, the first step in addressing grief is attending to the basics—rest, nourishment, and care. God didn't chastise Elijah for his despair; He gently sustained him.

God also spoke to Elijah, not in the dramatic fire or wind or earthquake Elijah might have expected, but in a gentle whisper (1 Kings 19:12). In that moment, God's still, small voice reaffirmed His presence and purpose for Elijah, reminding him that he was not alone. Seven thousand in Israel had not bowed to Baal, and Elijah's mission was not over.

Elijah's story shows us that even spiritual giants face moments of grief and despair. His journey through the wilderness reminds us that God doesn't abandon us in our lowest moments. Instead, He meets us there—providing for our needs, listening to our cries, and gently calling us forward into His purposes. Elijah's grief didn't disqualify him; it deepened his dependence on the God who walks with us, even in the wilderness.

Silent Cry For Justice

Tamar's story stands as one of the most heartbreaking narratives in Scripture—a raw account of betrayal, abuse, and the shattering aftermath of a violation that left her isolated and deeply wounded. Found in 2 Samuel 13, Tamar's experience lays bare the profound anguish that follows injustice and the sorrow of having one's dignity and innocence stolen.

The story begins with Amnon, Tamar's half-brother, consumed by lust and plotting to take what he wanted. Feigning illness, Amnon lured Tamar into his room under the guise of needing her care. What should have been a safe space—a family member's home—became a place of unspeakable violation. After assaulting her, Amnon's feelings turned to loathing, and he cast her out with cruelty, adding rejection to her trauma.

Tamar's response is a vivid depiction of grief and shame. She tore her richly ornamented robe, the symbol of her dignity and status as a king's daughter, and placed ashes on her head. These actions were outward signs of her inner devastation. Her lament was not just for the crime against her but for the loss of her sense of safety, honor, and identity.

The text tells us that Tamar "put her hands on her head and went away, weeping aloud as she went" (2 Samuel 13:19). Can you feel the weight of her sorrow? The humiliation and betrayal were compounded by the silence that followed. Though her brother Absalom took her into his home, the lack of justice for her pain must have deepened her anguish. David, her father, heard what had happened but did nothing to hold Amnon accountable, a failure that must have left Tamar feeling utterly forsaken.

Tamar's story illustrates a grief that many survivors of abuse can relate to—a grief marked by profound loneliness and a sense of abandonment. The text says that Tamar "lived in her brother Absalom's house, a desolate woman" (2 Samuel 13:20). The word "desolate" captures the devastation of her heart and the hopelessness of her situation. Tamar's grief was not only for what happened but for what would never be. Her future, as she had envisioned it, was gone.

For those who have experienced betrayal or trauma, Tamar's story resonates deeply. It acknowledges the rawness of pain and the injustice that so often accompanies it. I understand the sensitivity of including Tamar's story in this context. For those who have faced similar pain, Tamar's story may stir memories and emotions that are difficult to bear. Yet her story also reminds us that God sees the brokenhearted. Though Tamar's cries were met with silence from those around her, they were not unheard by the One who is near to the crushed in spirit (Psalm 34:18).

In Tamar's grief, we also find a call to care for and advocate for those who have been hurt. Her story challenges us to not look away from pain, to pursue justice for the vulnerable, and to extend compassion and support to the desolate. For survivors reading her story, Tamar's life is a testament that your pain is seen, your voice matters, and your healing is important.

Even though Tamar's story in Scripture doesn't show resolution, we serve a God who promises to bring ultimate justice and redemption. For every tear shed in anguish, there is hope in a God who binds up the broken-hearted and restores what has been lost (Isaiah 61:1-3).

The Tension Of Faith And Grief

Faith and grief—two forces that often feel at odds with each other, pulling us in different directions. On the one hand, we want to trust God and believe in His goodness and sovereignty. On the other hand, loss hits us like a freight train, leaving us breathless, angry, and questioning everything we thought we knew about Him. Is it okay to feel this way? Is it okay to grieve deeply and still call yourself a person of faith?

Let me tell you a story.

There was a woman—let's call her Lily—who gave birth to a stillborn baby. While confiding in her pastor, she told him that her family and friends kept saying things like, "God has a plan," or, "Your baby's in a better place now." Lily said she wanted to scream every time she heard those words. Not because she didn't believe in heaven but because those platitudes felt like they were asking her to bypass her pain. At the same time, she felt guilty for feeling so much anger toward God. She said, "If I trust Him, shouldn't I feel peace? Shouldn't I stop crying already?" Her story is the tension we're talking about—the tightrope between faith and grief.

Is it okay to question God? The answer, resoundingly, is yes. Scripture is full of examples of faithful people who brought their deepest questions, doubts, and even anger to God. The psalmists cried out, "How long, Lord? Will you forget me forever?" (Psalm 13:1). Jeremiah accused God of deceiving him (Jeremiah 20:7).

And let's not forget Job, who didn't hold back his frustrations. God is not afraid of our questions. He doesn't flinch at our doubt or recoil at our anger. Instead, He invites us to bring our raw, unfiltered emotions to Him. As Jesus said in Matthew 5:4, "Blessed are those who mourn, for they will be comforted." Mourning is not a lack of faith—it's a deeply human response to loss. It's the doorway to the comfort Jesus promises.

Lily's guilt for her grief is something many people feel. Somewhere along the way, we've bought into the idea that faith means having it all together—that if we truly trust God, we'll skip over the hard feelings and land straight in joy. But that's not what the Bible teaches. Here's the paradox: You can trust God completely and still feel the weight of your loss. Faith and grief aren't enemies; they're companions on the same journey. Grieving doesn't mean you don't believe in God's goodness—it means you're human. And it's in our humanity that God meets us.

Later, Lily said of her season of deep grief, "I thought I was failing in my faith because I couldn't stop crying. But what I realized is that every tear I cried brought me closer to God. I stopped trying to fight my grief and started bringing it to Him instead."

That's the key. **Grief isn't something to get over; it's something to bring to God.** He's the one who promises to comfort us, to walk with us through the valley, and to turn our mourning into joy—not by erasing our pain, but by redeeming it.

So, if you're walking the tightrope of faith and grief, let yourself feel the tension. Let yourself weep and trust, question, and believe. God is big enough to hold it all. And as you hold on to Him, you'll find He's holding on to you even tighter.

The Healing Journey

Grief isn't a straight road or something to be fixed— it's a uniquely personal experience, unfolding in its own time and way. While there's no universal roadmap, there are practices that can help you navigate the valleys of sorrow and begin to find healing. These steps aren't about rushing through the pain but learning to carry it with honesty, grace, and hope.

Lament: Honest Communication With God

Lament is one of the most powerful tools for processing grief—a raw, unfiltered conversation with God about your pain. The Bible is rich with examples of lament, particularly in the Psalms. David and other psalmists often cried out to God in their darkest moments, expressing anger, sorrow, and confusion. In Psalm 13, David begins with, "How long, Lord? Will you forget me forever?"

but ends with a declaration of trust: "But I trust in your unfailing love" (Psalm 13:1, 5).

Lament is not about finding instant answers; it's about being honest with God. It's saying, "This hurts, and I don't understand, but I'm bringing it to You." Don't let that religious voice inside your head keep you from processing your pain honestly with God. He is not offended by your questions or your pain. He invites you to pour it out before Him because He's the only one who can truly carry it.

Community: Letting Others Walk Alongside You

Grief can feel isolating, but it was never meant to be carried alone. Paul reminds us in Galatians 6:2, "Carry each other's burdens, and in this way you will fulfill the law of Christ." The people God places in your life— friends, family, your church community—are there to help you shoulder the weight of loss.

Letting others in can be hard, especially when you're in the thick of grief. You might feel like a burden or worry that others won't understand. But community is a gift, a tangible reminder of God's presence through His people. Whether it's a friend sitting silently with you, a meal delivered to your doorstep, or someone faithfully praying for you, these acts of love anchor you in the truth that you are not alone.

Time and Patience: Healing Is A Journey

Grief is not something you "get over." It's something

you learn to carry, and that takes time. Ecclesiastes 3 reminds us that there is "a time to weep and a time to laugh, a time to mourn and a time to dance" (Ecclesiastes 3:4). Your timeline might look different from someone else's, and that's okay.

Be patient with yourself. Healing is a process, not a sprint. Some days, you may feel a glimmer of hope; other days, the weight of loss may feel unbearable again. Both are part of the journey. Give yourself permission to grieve at your own pace, trusting that God is with you in every step, no matter how small.

Counseling and Prayer: Seeking Help and Support

Sometimes, the weight of grief feels too heavy to carry alone, even with the support of friends and family. That's where counseling and prayer come in. Seeking help from a therapist or pastor doesn't mean your faith is weak—it means you're taking a brave step toward healing.

Christian counseling, in particular, integrates biblical truths with psychological tools to help you process your emotions and find hope in God's promises. Prayer, whether with a trusted friend, a pastor, or in your private time with God, invites His healing presence into your pain. James 5:16 reminds us, "Pray for each other so that you may be healed. The prayer of a righteous person is powerful and effective."

Seeking support through local churches or organizations that offer grief support groups can be a lifeline during seasons of loss. Many churches host groups specifically designed to walk alongside those navigating the pain of grief, providing a safe space to share your story and connect with others who understand. These groups often combine emotional support with biblical encouragement, offering practical healing tools and reminders of God's presence in your sorrow.

Beyond churches, community organizations and counseling centers frequently host grief support programs, ensuring that no one has to walk the journey of loss alone. Reaching out may feel like a leap of faith, but it can lead to comfort, connection, and hope.

Grief is complex and often overwhelming, but these practices—lament, community, patience, and seeking help—can guide you through the storm. They won't erase the pain, but they will help you carry it in a way that leads to healing, hope, and deeper trust in the God who sees your tears and promises to one day wipe them all away.

The Bitter And The Sweet

Grief and joy might seem like opposites, but they often share space in the same moment. Grief doesn't disappear when joy appears, and joy doesn't cancel out grief. Instead, they intertwine, shaping the complexity of our human experience. The sharp ache of loss sits right beside the soft glow of joy as it slowly returns.

A common misunderstanding about grief is the idea that joy can only come once grief is over, as if healing demands we leave sorrow behind. The truth is more layered. Over time, gratitude and hope can grow amid loss. This doesn't mean the pain vanishes or the memory fades. It means that, alongside sorrow, joy can find room to grow.

Joy doesn't mean forgetting the pain of loss—it helps us notice the good that's still around us. Grief can sharpen our eyes to small blessings: a kind word, the warmth of sunlight, or a child's laughter. Gratitude for these moments isn't about "moving on." It's about seeing goodness even in the shadows.

Faith helps us hold grief and joy together. The Psalms often reflect this tension. Psalm 30:5 says, "Weeping may stay for the night, but rejoicing comes in the morning." The psalmist doesn't deny sorrow but affirms joy's return. Faith doesn't pretend pain isn't real—it gives us the strength to carry it without being overwhelmed.

Some of the most powerful examples come from those who channel their grief into love. A parent who has lost a child might create something meaningful in their memory, turning their sorrow into hope for others. Their joy in making a difference doesn't erase their loss but complements it, forming a richer story of healing.

Finding joy in the midst of grief isn't about pretending the pain isn't real. It's about letting God meet you in both your tears and your smiles. It's about trusting Him to hold the tension of life's bittersweet moments. And it's about leaning into the promise that grief isn't the final word. The God who brings beauty from ashes will also bring joy, even in the middle of sorrow.

An Eternal Perspective

Grief has a way of sharpening our awareness of the world's brokenness. It strips away illusions of control, permanence, and safety, forcing us to face the reality that life is not as it should be. But even as grief lays bare our vulnerability, it also points us to a greater hope—the promise of resurrection and restoration in Christ.

It's in this tension, between the pain of the present and the hope of eternity, that we find the perspective to keep going. The sorrow we feel today is temporary, even though it doesn't feel that way. The ache in our hearts reminds us that this world isn't our final home and that God is working toward a glorious redemption where all wrongs are made right.

Grief also serves a deeper purpose in shaping us. It's not that God causes our pain—far from it—but He never wastes it. In Romans 5:3-4, Paul writes that "suffering produces perseverance; perseverance, character; and character, hope." This doesn't mean we gloss over our pain with platitudes. It means that God, in His infinite kindness, meets us in our suffering and uses it to draw us closer to Him. God molds our faith into something more resilient, more authentic in the wrestling, the crying out, and even the silence.

Grief is not the end of the story. It is a chapter, albeit a difficult one, in the narrative of redemption. The hope of resurrection reminds us that even though loss marks us, it doesn't define us. Like Christ's, our scars become reminders not of defeat but of victory—evidence of the God who brings beauty from ashes and life from death. In the darkest valleys of grief, we hold onto this eternal perspective, trusting that what we endure now pales in comparison to the glory that awaits us (Romans 8:18). This hope doesn't erase our sorrow but gives it context, anchoring us in the unshakable truth of God's love and the promise of restoration.

Grief, though deeply painful, holds within it the seeds of transformation. It has a way of slowing us down, forcing us to confront what truly matters, and inviting us into deeper dependence on God. It's not a gift we would choose, but one that can shape us profoundly if we allow it. Grief strips away our illusions of self-sufficiency and reminds us of our need for the One who walks with us in the darkest valleys.

Grief doesn't mean we're abandoned or forgotten. Instead, it can be an intimate space where God does His most tender work. It may not make sense at the moment, but in time, grief can deepen our empathy, strengthen our faith, and even point us to the hope of resurrection—a reminder that the pain of this world is temporary, but God's promises are eternal.

A Prayer For The Grieving

Take a moment to talk to God:

> *Father, You know the depths of my sorrow, the ache in my heart, and the questions that feel unanswered. Thank You for being close to me in this valley, for Your promise never to leave or forsake me. Help me to trust You, even when I can't see the way forward. Use this pain to draw me closer to You and to deepen my faith. Fill me with hope, Lord—the hope of Your presence now and the hope of restoration to come. Amen.*

If prayer feels difficult right now, take a moment to write down what you're feeling. Bring those raw, un-filtered thoughts to God, knowing He welcomes your honesty. Grief is a journey; wherever you are on that path, remember that you are not alone. God is with you, and His love will sustain you.

Andrea's Story

There are moments in life that catch you off guard, altering your world in an instant—forever. That was what happened to me on November 11, 2021.

I woke up early that morning, excited about a trip to visit my grandma for her birthday. As I got ready with my husband, Vernick, we talked about the weeks ahead—holiday preparations, work schedules, and everyday plans. Before we went our separate ways for the day (since he was staying behind for work), we exchanged our usual I love you's and shared a kiss. I remember pausing for a moment, something in me urging, Give him one more kiss. So I did. Unknowingly, that was the last moment we would share together on this side of heaven.

Less than three hours later, I found myself in a hospital waiting room—numb, panicked, terrified. Every emotion imaginable raced through me as I paced and prayed, my mind a whirlwind of desperate thoughts. Looking out the window, I was suddenly reminded of Matthew 10:29-31: "Not one sparrow falls to the ground outside the Father's care."

At that moment, I felt God's overwhelming peace. Deep in my spirit, I knew Vernick was okay, and somehow, I would be too. Even in the midst of fear and confusion, I trusted that God held us both in the palm of His hand—because His love is that great. I continued to pray, clinging to His promises, until the doctor walked in and confirmed what I already knew. Vernick was no longer here in the physical—he was with Jesus.

The first few weeks were a blur. Each morning, I woke up having to remind myself of what had happened, still in disbelief that my seemingly healthy, 37-year-old husband of 12 years was gone. I'd be lying if I said I didn't wrestle with anger—the why me? questions. I would hear others complain about their spouses and want to scream, both at them and at God. Vernick and I had a strong marriage, we loved each other deeply, we worshiped Jesus together, and we served Him faithfully—why did it have to be him? That was the raw, human part of me, the honest thoughts I wrestled with. But as I poured my heart out to Jesus, I felt His gentle touch, steadying me, reminding me that His ways are not my ways. In my pain, I found shelter under the shadow of His wing.

I remember one morning vividly, about two to three months after losing Vernick, when I was on a trip to Colorado with a friend. I had gone for a few days to get away and enjoy nature—there are few things more healing to me than spending time with God in His creation. That morning, I woke up, and the emptiness and loneliness were practically tangible. It was like a dark shadow covered me in that room, and I felt the heaviness of grief in a way I didn't know was possible.

Immediately, the Holy Spirit brought Psalm 23 to my mind: "Yea, though I walk through the valley of the shadow of death, I will fear no evil; for You are with me." I cried, prayed, and thanked Him for that reminder. Then, when I opened my Bible app to read, wouldn't you know—the verse of the day was the very one that had been impressed on me as soon as I woke up? At that moment, I realized I was encountering the nearness of God in a new and very real way. He was going to be walking alongside me through this. For every moment of doubt or insecurity, Jesus would remind me of who He was. He had been faithful before, and He would remain faithful now.

That first year was full of milestones—holidays, birthdays, anniversaries—each one carrying the sharp pangs of grief. But time and again, God provided just what I needed: the right person, the right word, the right reminder. When it felt like too much, I would cry out to Him, and He was always there in the middle of the mess. My grief wasn't perfect, and my healing was far from linear, but in His hands, even my brokenness became something beautiful. He continued to be the Redeemer He has always been.

I read books about grief, followed widows further along in their journey, attended counseling and grief support groups, stayed connected to church, and spent time with friends. Each of these things helped in its own way. But nothing brought healing like sitting with Jesus in the heaviness of it all. Learning how to cope was good. Processing was necessary. But a single moment with Him—brought peace of mind, a shift in perspective, and realigned thinking. He was my portion. He was enough.

I would often encounter Him most on my runs. While it was great for my physical health, by far, it contributed most to my mental and spiritual health. It was just me and Jesus in His creation, listening to worship songs—sometimes on repeat—that spoke God's truth over my life. I found a new appreciation for David and the Psalms—the back-and-forth between praise and lament. God, You are so worthy… but why have You abandoned me? It might sound contradictory, but it was real and raw. I knew God could handle my honesty, even when it sounded like I doubted Him. As I laid my heart bare in my pain—deep, excruciating pain—His presence met me with the unshakable truth: He was still good. Even if things didn't turn out how I wanted them, I would praise Him because I was unequivocally convinced of His goodness and worthiness.

I have since met an amazing man who gives respect and honor to the role Vernick had in my life—not threatened, but filled with compassion. That, in and of itself, is a testament to God's redeeming nature. He knew my heart's desire, and in His timing, provided the sweetest gift through him.

Now that I'm over three years removed from losing Vernick, the memories have become more sweet than bitter. I get to carry that love with me every day. In a strange way, I'm thankful for experiencing the Valley of the Shadow of Death. Don't misunderstand me—I'm not thankful for losing Vernick. I miss him every day, and I'm sure I always will. But the assurance and relationship I now have with God—His presence in my life—nothing can take that away. I have learned and truly experienced that even when it hurts the most and my life is turned upside down, I can trust His promises. That He is good. He is faithful. He is close to the brokenhearted. He is my Redeemer, my Provider, my Friend.

Love and grief—the former necessitates the latter. It's a beautiful, painful part of the human experience. I look back now and realize how blessed I am to have experienced it in its fullness. Nothing is wasted.

CHAPTER SIX

SUFFERING IN COMMUNITY

As I shared at the beginning of this book, one year into our marriage, I was diagnosed with cancer. I'll never forget the look on my wife Bethany's face as I woke up from the biopsy. The doctor had already spoken to her while I was still under anesthesia, telling her that he was almost certain of the diagnosis and that the pathology report would likely confirm it. When I came to, Bethany gently told me the doctor would be coming in to talk to me. Her face said it all—she'd already been crying.

What followed was a whirlwind of surgeries, consultations, and preparing for chemotherapy. We were young, overwhelmed, and trying to process the enormity of it all. Living over an hour away from the treatment center added another layer of difficulty. It didn't take long for us to realize that as much as we wanted to handle everything on our own, we couldn't. We needed help.

At first, we hesitated to inconvenience anyone. But the love and support that poured out from our family and church community caught us completely off guard. Meals started arriving at our doorstep. People sent cards, money, and notes of encouragement.

I'll never forget the moment one man handed us an envelope—we found a check for $5,000 inside when we opened it later. His wife had fought her own battle with cancer, and he understood firsthand the weight of the journey we were embarking on. His gift wasn't just generous—it was deeply empathetic, born out of shared experience and a heart that knew exactly what we were facing. For two newlyweds drowning in medical bills, that $5,000 check might as well have been a million dollars. Such an incredible act of generosity floored us.

And when Bethany couldn't always take off work to drive me to my chemo appointments, others in the church stepped up without hesitation. People we weren't even that close to volunteered their time, their gas, and their hearts to make sure we weren't walking through this alone. It was incredible.

The kindness of those people humbled us. They didn't just help—they carried us. Each act of love, whether big or small, reminded us that we weren't abandoned in our suffering. Those moments of sacrifice and generosity left a permanent mark on me. I'll never forget how little community surrounded us during one of the hardest seasons of our lives. I'll always be grateful.

The only thing worse than suffering is suffering alone. But the good news is that you don't have to. The family of God exists as a source of strength, encouragement, and healing in our darkest moments. Community doesn't erase the pain, but it lightens the load when others come alongside us, offering their presence and care. This chapter explores why community is vital in suffering, how we can lean into it, and how we can be the hands and feet of Jesus for others who are hurting.

When Pain Finds A Village

Suffering isolates. It pulls us inward, tempting us to close off from others and carry the burden alone. We tell ourselves we don't want to be a bother or admit we need help. It feels easier—or at least less vulnerable—to rely on ourselves rather than lean on others. But God didn't design us to face life's hardships in solitude. He created us for connection, and that need becomes especially clear in seasons of pain. The Apostle Paul reminds us in Galatians 6:2, "Carry each other's burdens, and in this way, you will fulfill the law of Christ." This isn't just a suggestion; it's part of how God intends for His people to love and support one another.

Our old friend Job understood the loneliness of suffering. Reflecting on the lack of support from his friends, he laments, "My brothers are as undependable as intermittent streams, as the streams that overflow" (Job 6:15). And that's a point to lean into. Sometimes, even the people closest to us fail to provide the support we desperately need. Their words can feel empty, their actions insufficient, and their absence more glaring than ever. When we're in the depths of pain, these disappointments can cut deeply, amplifying our hurt and pushing us further into isolation.

Even when people get it wrong—and they often will—it's worth pursuing grace for those who struggle to support us. I've come to understand something valuable about people, especially in the way they respond to the suffering of others. Some seem to have an almost instinctive ability to show up at just the right moment. They say the words you didn't even realize you needed to hear, or they quietly offer the kind of help that eases your burden without adding to it. These people are a gift, and their actions feel like grace in the middle of chaos.

But not everyone is wired that way. Some people genuinely care but freeze when faced with the pain of others. It's not because they're indifferent or unkind—they just don't know what to do or say. And that uncertainty can feel paralyzing. They hesitate, unsure how to step in or if their efforts will be welcomed. Often, the worse the suffering, the more anxiety they feel about getting it wrong. What if they say the wrong thing? What if their attempts to help only add to the pain? That fear of making things worse can hold them back, even when their presence alone could be a comfort.

And while it's easy to feel hurt or overlooked when people don't show up the way we need, I've learned that this hesitation often has nothing to do with a lack of love or care. In fact, their silence can come from caring too much and not wanting to add to the weight of your pain. This realization has helped me approach those moments with grace, choosing to believe the best about the people around me—even when their actions, or lack thereof, don't meet my expectations.

Of course, some may minimize or even dismiss your suffering, often with comments like, "Well, at least it's not as bad as what poor Jim is going through." It's frustrating, even hurtful, to feel like your pain is being trivialized. But I've realized that this kind of response often stems from their own unresolved struggles. Many people haven't learned how to process their pain, so when confronted with someone else's suffering, they default to comparison or deflection.

It's not necessarily a lack of care; it's a lack of understanding or an inability to sit with discomfort. They might genuinely believe they're helping by putting things into perspective, even if their words miss the mark entirely. Recognizing this doesn't take away the sting, but it can help you not to take it personally. Their response says more about their need for growth than about the validity of your pain. Offer grace where you can, and try to surround yourself with those willing to meet you where you are without judgment or comparison.

The truth is that everyone responds to suffering differently.

Some leap into action, while others need guidance or reassurance that their small efforts matter. But I've come to understand that even when someone's response isn't perfect—or when it's absent altogether—it doesn't mean their heart isn't in the right place. Sometimes, they're just as overwhelmed by your pain as you are. Learning to give grace in those moments has been one of the hardest but most freeing lessons in my own journeys through suffering.

Grieving With Those Who Grieve

It's one thing to receive comfort; it's another to extend it to others. As Christians, we're called to walk alongside those who are grieving, facing illness, or enduring loss. But let's be honest—it's not always easy. Pain is messy, and stepping into someone else's suffering can feel intimidating, especially when we're unsure of what to say or do. Yet, Scripture and psychological insight offer us valuable guidance for how to truly walk with others in their hardest moments.

Job's friends give us a clear example of how not to care for someone who is suffering. They started well—they showed up and sat in silence for seven days, mourning with him (Job 2:13). The problem is that they felt the need to open their mouths and express their opinion. When Job began to express his anguish, his friends didn't respond with compassion or understanding.

Instead, they turned to accusations, convinced that Job's suffering must be his fault. Their worldview couldn't reconcile Job's pain with their belief in a strict system of retribution: blessings for the righteous, curses for the wicked. Eliphaz insinuated, "Consider now: Who, being innocent, has ever perished? Where were the upright ever destroyed?" (Job 4:7). In their minds, Job's suffering was evidence of hidden sin, and they felt it their duty to correct him.

This response only added to Job's pain. Already burdened by his grief, Job was now forced to defend his character to the people who were supposed to support him. His blunt rebuke in Job 16:2 lays bare his disappointment: "I have heard many things like these; you are miserable comforters, all of you!" Have you ever been "comforted" by someone like these guys? Then you can surely sympathize with Job here.

Henri Nouwen's insights on care resonate deeply here:

> *Real care excludes indifference and is the opposite of apathy… The basic meaning of care is to grieve, to experience sorrow, to cry out with.*

See, Job's friends failed because they didn't stay in that space of shared grief. Instead of entering Job's sorrow with him, they distanced themselves, opting for judgment rather than compassion. Their inability to truly see Job's pain—choosing instead to filter it through their own limited theological framework—turned their care into condemnation.

The story of Job's friends is a cautionary tale for all of us. It's a reminder that when someone is suffering, our first and most crucial response should be to listen, empathize, and simply be present. Even well-meaning explanations can feel hollow and dismissive in the face of deep pain. As Paul writes in Romans 12:15, "Rejoice with those who rejoice; mourn with those who mourn." True comfort begins when we enter into another's sorrow without judgment or the need to fix it. It's in that shared space of vulnerability and grace that healing can begin.

The Ministry Of Presence

Theology and psychology agree on this: true care begins with presence. Again, Henri Nouwen, in *Out of Solitude*, writes, "Caring means entering into the experience of another—not standing at a distance offering advice but stepping into their sorrow, even if it costs you." This isn't just poetic sentiment; it's a profound truth that challenges our natural instincts to fix, solve, or rationalize someone's pain. The Apostle Paul captured this idea in his call to "mourn with those who mourn" (Romans 12:15). Real care doesn't attempt to tidy up someone's grief with explanations or solutions. Instead, it shares the weight of the burden, even when there's no immediate way to relieve it.

Research in psychology underscores the timeless wisdom that presence is the foundation of real care. Studies on emotional resilience consistently show that the presence of a supportive friend or family member during times of stress significantly reduces the psychological toll of trauma. In fact, perceived social support has been identified as one of the most critical factors in mitigating anxiety, depression, and other emotional repercussions following traumatic events.

Clinical psychologist Dr. Sue Johnson emphasizes the importance of emotional attunement in her work on attachment theory. Emotional attunement, she explains, involves not only being physically present but also fully engaging emotionally with the person in distress. This kind of presence creates what Johnson calls a "safe haven."

A safe haven provides a relational environment where someone can process their grief, fear, or pain without feeling judged or abandoned. Johnson's groundbreaking research demonstrates that such environments dramatically improve emotional recovery and foster resilience, even during prolonged suffering.

The power of presence extends beyond mere proximity. It's about conveying, both through words and actions, a message of solidarity and love. As Dr. Bessel van der Kolk notes in *The Body Keeps the Score*, "Being able to feel safe with other people is probably the single most important aspect of mental health. Safe connections are fundamental to meaningful and satisfying lives." When people feel seen, heard, and cared for, their ability to cope with adversity increases exponentially.

This insight has profound implications for how we walk with others through their suffering. Words of advice or quick-fix solutions often pale in comparison to the healing power of simply being there. People may not always remember the specific words spoken during their darkest moments, but they almost always remember the presence of those who stood with them in the storm.

The human brain is wired for connection. Neuroscience confirms that in times of distress, the presence of a calm and supportive individual can even regulate the nervous system, reducing the fight-or-flight response and helping a person return to a state of emotional balance. In other words, your quiet presence can be a lifeline for someone drowning in pain.

Think about the moments when you've felt most vulnerable or broken. Did someone's advice or platitudes bring comfort? Probably not. What likely made the difference was the presence of someone who didn't shy away from your pain—someone who showed up and stayed, even when they didn't have the perfect words to say. That kind of presence is rare and precious, and it's exactly what theology and psychology both affirm as the essence of care.

When Lazarus died, Jesus didn't begin with a theological discourse about the resurrection. He wept. He stepped fully into the grief of Mary and Martha, sharing their tears before He offered any hope of a miracle (John 11:35). His presence validated their pain, showing them—and us—that God doesn't stand aloof from our suffering but meets us in it.

This is the challenge and beauty of real care. It's not about having the right answers or even the ability to change someone's circumstances. It's about showing up, staying close, and being willing to bear the weight of someone else's sorrow. In many ways, it reflects the incarnation: God stepping into human history, taking on flesh, and walking alongside us in our pain.

Psychologist Brené Brown has written extensively about the power of empathy, noting that "empathy fuels connection; sympathy drives disconnection." Sympathy stands at a distance, offering pity or advice. On the other hand, empathy draws near, saying, "I'm here. I don't have all the answers, but I'll sit with you in this." Brown's research echoes the biblical principle that care begins not with words but with presence—a willingness to step into the discomfort of someone else's story and simply be there.

For Christians, this idea of costly care should resonate deeply. We follow a Savior who bore the ultimate cost to draw near to us in our suffering. His model challenges us to do the same for others. It's not always easy—walking with someone through grief, illness, or loss can be emotionally draining and even painful. But as Nouwen reminds us, "When we honestly ask ourselves which person in our lives means the most to us, we often find that it is those who, instead of giving much advice, solutions, or cures, have chosen rather to share our pain and touch our wounds with a gentle and tender hand."

This is so true. When I look back on my cancer journey as a young man, it's the people who drove me to my treatments that stand out the most. They sat beside me for hours while I reclined in the treatment chair, the nurse steadily administering the medications. Then they'd drive me home, often in near silence. I don't remember much of the advice or even the words of encouragement people gave me during that time. What stays with me, though, are the faces of those who simply showed up and sat with me. Their quiet presence spoke volumes—far more than any words ever could.

Ultimately, the ministry of presence is not about perfection but faithfulness. It's about being willing to sit in the tension of unanswered questions, unresolved pain, and unfixable problems. It's about embodying the love of Christ, who not only wept with those who wept but also carried their sorrows to the cross. Whether through a silent vigil by a hospital bed, a hug that speaks volumes, or simply showing up again and again, we have the opportunity to reflect God's love in a way that words alone never could.

This is the heart of real care: not fixing but walking alongside.

It's messy and imperfect, but it's also transformative.

For those who give it and for those who receive it, the ministry of presence is a sacred space where healing begins, burdens are shared, and hope quietly takes root.

How To Bear A Burden

It's a verse many of us know by heart, but how often do we stop to think about what it really means? What does it look like to "carry" someone else's burdens? Is it lending a listening ear, offering practical help, or simply being present?

Walking with others in their suffering is both a privilege and a responsibility. It's one of the most tangible ways we reflect the love of Christ to those in need. This call is not about fixing people or solving their problems—it's about sharing the weight they're carrying, even if only for a little while. Just as Christ came alongside us in our brokenness, we're invited to do the same for others.

So, how do we live out this calling? It starts with intentionality. It means moving beyond good intentions to practical action. Here are a few practical steps to help us bear each other's burdens:

Pray for them. Prayer is not just a fallback when we're at a loss for what else to do—it's one of the most profound and powerful acts of love we can offer. In moments of suffering, when words fall short and solutions are out of reach, prayer becomes a bridge between human need and divine power. It's not a passive response but an active engagement in the spiritual realm for those we love.

Job, in the depths of his despair, longed for someone

to intercede for him, saying, "My intercessor is my friend as my eyes pour out tears to God; on behalf of a man he pleads with God as one pleads for a friend" (Job 16:20-21). The image is striking—a friend standing before God, pleading earnestly for mercy and intervention. Job's cry captures a deep truth: in suffering, the knowledge that someone is lifting you up in prayer can bring immeasurable comfort.

When you pray for someone, you do more than offer kind thoughts or empty platitudes. You're standing in the gap for them, bringing their burdens before the One who knows them better than anyone else. You're entrusting their pain, healing, and future to God's capable hands. And whether or not they feel the impact of your prayers immediately, your intercession sends a message—they are not forgotten by God or His people. In prayer, we acknowledge that the burden is too great for us to carry alone, and we entrust it to the One whose strength is limitless. This act of intercession becomes a lifeline—not only for the person you are praying for but also for you, as it roots your hope and confidence in God's faithfulness.

Prayer also transcends physical limitations. You may not be able to fix the problem, heal the hurt, or even be physically present with someone who is suffering—but prayer has no such boundaries. It reaches into hospital rooms, broken homes, and weary hearts, carrying the love of God to places we cannot go.

So pray boldly. Pray specifically. Lift up their needs, their fears, and their sorrows to God. Pray for their peace, their healing, and their hope. And even if your prayers seem small or inadequate, trust that they are part of something far greater—an outpouring of God's love that flows through His people. As James reminds us, "The prayer of a righteous person is powerful and effective" (James 5:16). When you intercede for someone, you participate in that power, joining in God's work of redemption and restoration.

Be Present. We have touched on this already, but the power of presence cannot be overstated. In a world so quick to offer advice, fix problems, or move on to the next task, simply showing up and sitting with someone in their pain is a rare gift. Presence speaks when words fail. It communicates, *"I see you. I'm with you. You're not alone."*

Jesus modeled this beautifully in His ministry. When Jairus' daughter was sick and ultimately died, He went to the house, took her by the hand, and brought her back to life (Mark 5:21-43). Before the miracle, though, He was present. He walked with Jairus through his fears and stood with the mourners in their grief. His presence was a source of hope and comfort even before the healing came.

Sometimes, showing up means going to a friend's house when they're too overwhelmed to reply to your texts. It could look like sitting in a hospital room for hours, saying nothing, just being there. Or maybe it's checking in weeks or even months after the initial crisis—long after everyone else has moved on.

Paul got this. Over and over in his letters, he emphasizes the power of being present for one another, whether in celebration or sorrow. In 2 Corinthians 1:4, he writes that God comforts us in our troubles so that "we can comfort those in any trouble with the comfort we ourselves receive from God."

Real comfort isn't about quick fixes or perfect answers; it's about showing up and standing with someone in their pain. Sometimes, silence says more than words ever could. A hand on their shoulder, crying with them, or simply sitting close can remind someone: *You're not alone. I'm here. And so is God.*

Be Patient. Grief doesn't come with an expiration date. Healing isn't linear, and no two people will process pain in the same way. For some, grief hits like a tidal wave, overwhelming and immediate. For others, it's a slow burn, creeping in when life quiets down. Either way, the journey through pain takes time, and that time looks different for everyone.

Resist the urge to rush someone through their grief, no matter how well-meaning your intentions might be. Comments like, "You'll feel better soon," or comparisons like, "I know exactly how you feel," can come off as dismissive—even if that's not your heart behind it. The truth is, you don't know exactly how they feel. Their pain is as unique as their fingerprint. Be patient with their questions, their silences, and even their anger. Don't try to clean up their grief or put it into tidy boxes. Sit with them in the mess, however long it takes.

Psychologists emphasize the importance of patience when supporting those facing trauma or loss. People need the space to process at their own pace without the added burden of feeling like they're "doing it wrong" or taking too long. When we push someone to "move on" or "cheer up," we risk adding feelings of shame or frustration to an already heavy load. Instead, give them room to wrestle, mourn, and heal in their own time.

And while you wait alongside them, extend grace. Grace for the moments when their grief looks nothing like what you expected. Grace for their raw emotions, their questions, and even their doubts. Trust that God is at work in ways you can't see—doing the kind of deep, transformative work in their hearts that only He can do. Healing will come in His perfect timing.

Walking With The Grieving

Supporting someone who is grieving is one of the most profound and compassionate acts we can offer, yet it's also one of the most challenging. The path of grief is deeply personal, often winding and unpredictable, and knowing how to walk alongside someone without overstepping or withdrawing can feel overwhelming. But the good news is that you don't have to have all the right answers—or any answers at all. Grief isn't solved; it's carried. And your role as a companion is simply to help shoulder the weight when someone feels they can't carry it alone.

Knowing what to say to someone in grief can feel like walking a tightrope. Many of us worry about saying the wrong thing, and in our nervousness, we either blurt out something unhelpful or avoid saying anything at all. Let's clear up some of the confusion.

Grief is messy, unpredictable, and deeply individual. What someone needs one day might not be what they need the next. That's why patience and consistency are so important when walking with someone in grief. Be the friend who checks in—not just in the days after the loss, but in the weeks, months, and even years that follow. Grief often feels most isolating after the initial flood of support fades. Remember important dates, like anniversaries or birthdays, and tell them you're still thinking of them. A simple text, a card, or a phone call can be a powerful reminder that they're not forgotten.

And don't rush their process. Meet them where they are, whether that's in tears, anger, or even moments of laughter. Let them grieve at their own pace and resist the urge to push them toward "closure" or a neatly packaged resolution.

Supporting someone through grief is not about having the perfect words or being the hero who saves the day. It's about showing up, staying present, and letting God work through you. You don't have to fix their pain; you just have to be willing to walk alongside them in it.

Remember, grief is a marathon, not a sprint. It requires endurance, compassion, and faithfulness. But as you journey with someone through their pain, you may find your own heart stretched and softened in the process. Grief shared is grief lightened, and the love of Christ becomes tangible in the spaces where we choose to walk together.

Watch Your Words. Words hold incredible power. They can be a balm for a wounded heart, or they can unintentionally deepen the pain. People don't need clichés in times of suffering—they need connection.

Yet, all too often, well-meaning phrases like "God won't give you more than you can handle" slip out of our mouths. The intention might be to encourage, but these words often land with a thud, feeling dismissive or even cruel to someone in the depths of grief.

Try to avoid dismissive phrases like "I know exactly how you feel" or "Everything happens for a reason." Even if your intentions are good, these words aren't helpful. Instead, acknowledge their pain directly. It's also okay to ask open-ended questions like, "How can I support you right now?" This lets them guide you toward what they need without feeling pressured to fit into your idea of comfort. And don't be afraid of silence. Sometimes, that is the place where healing needs to take place.

Here's the truth: suffering doesn't make sense, and trying to wrap it up in a neat theological bow can do more harm than good.

Pain is messy. Questions linger. Grief doesn't resolve itself with a tidy explanation. Instead of trying to solve the unsolvable, focus on simply acknowledging the hurt. A heartfelt "I'm so sorry you're going through this" or "I don't have the right words, but I'm here for you" can be a lifeline to someone drowning in sorrow.

You don't need to explain their suffering or attempt to justify it. Honestly, most explanations, however well-intentioned, miss the mark entirely. What they need isn't answers—they need presence. Your humility in admitting, "I don't know why this is happening, but I care," will resonate far more deeply than platitudes ever could.

Sit with them. Hold their hand. Let them cry. When you do speak, choose words that reflect the depth of their pain, not words that try to gloss over it. As Proverbs 25:11 says, "A word fitly spoken is like apples of gold in a setting of silver." Thoughtful, compassionate words can be a source of comfort, reminding them that they are not alone and that their pain is seen.

Grace For The Journey

Finally, I've learned that walking with others in their suffering and grief is one of the hardest and holiest things we can do. It stretches you, challenges you, and demands grace—not just for the person you're helping but for yourself, too. You won't always say or do the right thing, and that's okay. What matters is showing up. Sometimes, just being there—imperfect, unsure, but present—is the most loving thing you can offer. It's not about fixing the pain but reflecting the love of Jesus, the One who always shows up for us.

One of the hardest lessons I've learned in life—and, let's be honest, I'm still learning—is how to respect the seasons others are in, even when they don't match my own. Romans 12:15 puts it plainly: "Rejoice with those who rejoice; weep with those who weep." But let's be real: that's easier said than done.

When you're in a season of pain, the joy of others can feel like salt in a wound. Their celebrations, milestones, and laughter can seem like a spotlight on what you've lost or longed for. But here's the truth: their joy doesn't diminish your pain. It's not a competition. It's a different season. Bitterness can creep in when we start comparing, and bitterness doesn't just steal your joy—it isolates you. It makes it hard to see the good that's still present, even in the middle of your pain.

The reverse is just as important. When someone walks through sorrow, we can't demand that they pretend to be joyful just because we're in a good place. It's unfair—and unkind—to ask someone to set aside their grief to match our celebration. Respecting others' seasons means meeting people where they are, not where we want them to be.

This takes grace. Grace for others, and grace for yourself. It means rejoicing with a friend when they announce their engagement, even if your own heart aches from a breakup. It means sitting in silence with someone who's grieving, even when your own life feels full of blessings. It means holding space for the highs and lows of life, trusting that your season will shift in its own time, too.

This is the beauty of the body of Christ. We're not all meant to experience the same things simultaneously. Some of us are called to weep, while others are called to rejoice. And sometimes, we're called to do both at once. Respecting those seasons isn't just about avoiding bitterness or selfishness—it's about learning to love well. It's about recognizing that God is at work in every season, both in yours and theirs. And it's about trusting Him enough to walk alongside each other, even when our paths look different.

Suffering has a way of deepening our connection with each other and with God. When you walk through someone else's pain, you'll likely find your own faith stretched and strengthened. It's in these moments of vulnerability and compassion that we begin to understand God's love on a whole new level. Suffering may not feel like holy ground, but when we show up for each other, it absolutely becomes that.

Grace And Responsibility

Community is a two-way street. While we're called to walk with others in their suffering, we're also responsible for how we walk through our own. That means resisting the urge to let bitterness creep in when someone doesn't get it right. It means choosing to forgive when words sting or help doesn't come the way we'd hoped. People won't always know how to show up for us, but we can't let that drive us into isolation.

At the same time, we have to own our part. If our suffering results from our choices, healing starts with acknowledging that. But here's the good news: God meets us with grace even in the mess we create. His love doesn't waver because we've made mistakes, and neither does the love of the people He's placed in our lives—at least, not when they reflect His heart. Accepting that grace and being open to the help God sends is one of the hardest and most humbling parts of suffering, but it's also one of the most beautiful.

Community is His idea. It's His gift. And when we lean into it—when we let people carry us through our suffering and when we show up to carry others—it changes us. In those moments of shared pain and joy, we experience the heart of God in ways we never could on our own.

The family of God is not perfect, but it's a reflection of Him nonetheless. When we carry each other's burdens, when we grieve together and celebrate together, we're doing what Jesus Himself did—walking alongside the broken, loving the hurting, and pointing to a hope that doesn't fail. So whether you're in the thick of suffering or standing beside someone who is, know this: you're not alone. We're in this together, and that's exactly how God designed it.

Collin's Story

My faith has never been challenged like this before. I am
afraid, and things seem so dark. I feel like I am losing my
mind, and my only prayer is that You would help me func-
tion as a husband and a dad.
(Journal Entry: December 14th, 2021)

My chest tightened. My heart pounded so hard it was
jumping in my throat. My skin burned as if electricity
were surging through my veins. I gasped for air, convinced
I was dying.

"This is it," I thought. "I'm having a heart attack."

I woke my wife, stumbled downstairs, and called
1-1-9 (Taiwan's version of 9-1-1). Trying to explain my
symptoms in Chinese while panicking only made things

worse. After five frantic minutes—in which I accidentally told them I lived in Xinzhuang (a city name sounding like 'heart') instead of saying I was having a heart attack—the ambulance arrived. You can't imagine the frustration of doing Chinese lessons in my head while thinking I was dying.

At the hospital, they ran tests, and the doctor asked if I had drunk caffeine that night.

Caffeine? Wasn't my body shutting down? Wasn't this supposed to be serious? I was relieved to be alive—but I still had no idea what had just happened. And I thought it was over.

I was wrong.

Up until I turned 36, life felt easy. Everything came naturally to me. God had been faithful, and I had experienced few failures. I believed that life would only get bigger, better, and more exciting.

I even remember a night in a community group when someone asked, "What's your biggest fear?"

Without hesitation, I said, "Failure."

They looked at me and asked, "You mean, you've never failed at anything?"

I paused. And then it hit me—I couldn't think of a single defining moment in my life where I had failed. Looking back, I see how blinded I was by my own pride and arrogance. I had built my life on my potential, believing that if God called me to something, then I could accomplish it (not Christ through me, but me).

And then 2021 came.

My family and I had been living in Taiwan, where we had planted a church in Taipei. While Taiwan initially handled the pandemic better than most, burnout and mental health struggles skyrocketed. Aside from COVID, living in another culture—while beautiful and formational—can cause stressors that I was blind to. For example, living under the semi-constant threat of a foreign invasion.

In my little corner of the world, we had a two-year-old church plant, three young kids, and I was in school full-time. I hadn't had a proper vacation in years.

But I thought I was fine. I believed I had no limitations. This mentality of neglecting my soul at the expense of what I was accomplishing is what led to multiple panic attacks and a full-blown nervous breakdown.

Over the next few months, the panic attacks decreased, and I assumed life would return to normal. So, I kept pushing forward—no rest, no slowing down. But anxiety has a way of finding cracks in the foundation.

That summer, Taiwan went into full lockdown. Church moved online, all three kids were home 24/7, and we experienced a major loss in the family. Stress compounded. I thought I was handling it well—until my wife and I visited a sleep doctor.

After running tests, the doctor looked at me and said, "You are carrying three times the stress of the average person."

Three times? How was that possible?

I had ignored the warning signs, and now my body was

shutting down. Anger, unforgiveness, and relentless stress had taken their toll. Adding to the pressure, we were also navigating a difficult situation with one of our children, which transformed our home from a place of refuge into a pressure cooker.

Thankfully, those around me saw the breakdown before I did, and I was forced into a two-month period of rest. I will be forever grateful to the men who called me to this.

That's when everything began to unravel.

The first month of rest was brutal. Cue the journal entry listed above. I felt like I was drowning, barely keeping my head above water. The panic attacks were replaced with something worse—a deep, gnawing doubt.

Faith had always come easily. Now, every prayer felt empty. Reading Scripture was anxiety-inducing. I questioned everything I had once been so sure of.

I thought *I'm a church planter—this isn't supposed to happen to me!* But doubt doesn't discriminate. It latches onto whatever is most sacred to you and shakes it.

I became obsessed with every intrusive thought. I spiraled into fear, constantly seeking reassurance. First, it was my health (Am I dying? What's this pain? Do I have a disease?), but soon it spread to my faith (What if everything I've staked my life on isn't true? What if God isn't real?).

Doubt became a relentless woodpecker in my mind, chipping away at the faith I once thought was unshakable. This doubt revealed that I had projected all my desires onto God, and when life became unfair, I started questioning His goodness.

Anxiety rarely stays in one place. It shifts. It morphs. It demands assurance about things that haven't even happened yet.

Here are some of my actual worries over the past few years:

- What if I have a heart attack?

- What if I have stomach cancer?

- What if I have ALS?

- What if I lose my faith?

- What if I lose control?

None of these things have happened. But anxiety doesn't care—it begs for tomorrow's grace today.

Yet God never promises tomorrow's grace today. He only promises enough for this moment. And when I demand guarantees about the future, I miss out on the peace He offers right now.

I keep thinking about Jacob.

> *So Jacob was left alone, and a man wrestled with him till daybreak... When the man saw that he could not overpower him, he touched the socket of Jacob's hip so that his hip was wrenched as he wrestled with the man.* (Genesis 32)

God crippled Jacob. For the rest of his life, he had a limp—a constant reminder of his encounter with God and the way God changed him.

I imagine there were days when Jacob hated that limp. It probably slowed him down and made simple tasks harder. And yet, it became part of his transformation.

In my life, I see now that God allows the crippling so He can do the crowning.

Since that season in late 2021, I can't begin to express how the Lord has given to me in suffering what I could never have understood through comfort. As someone once said, "The bitter is making me better."

Jesus isn't just an idea or a concept that we mentally assent to, but a person we are called to trust. I still have bouts of anxiety. We are still in a hard season as parents, but we know that God will use our suffering to make us more like Him.

CHAPTER SEVEN

WARFARE IN SUFFERING

S uffering isn't just painful—it's revealing. It pushes us to our limits, exposing what's hidden in our hearts and forcing us to confront the raw realities of our faith. In those moments, we're faced with a choice: will suffering break us, or will it shape us? The fight isn't just about our comfort or circumstances; it's about the condition of our souls.

The Bible often talks about suffering as a refining process. Peter writes, "These [trials] have come so that the proven genuineness of your faith—of greater worth than gold—may result in praise, glory, and honor when Jesus Christ is revealed" (1 Peter 1:7). Trials strip away the surface-level stuff and leave us staring at what's real. They reveal what we truly believe about God, ourselves, and the world.

But suffering isn't just a test—it's a battlefield. The

enemy is quick to take advantage of our pain, whispering lies that God doesn't care, that we're alone, or that we're not strong enough to make it through. He wants to sow bitterness, doubt, and despair. Yet Scripture reminds us that trials are also opportunities for growth. James writes, "Blessed is the one who perseveres under trial because, having stood the test, that person will receive the crown of life that the Lord has promised to those who love him" (James 1:12).

Suffering forces us to wrestle with hard questions: Is God really good? Does He care about me? Can He bring anything good out of this pain? It's in the wrestling that our faith is forged—or fractured. The pressure of suffering can crush us or press us closer to Christ.

This is a road believers have walked for centuries. Some have come out stronger, their faith refined like steel in fire. Others have struggled, and some have even walked away. But the beauty of the gospel is this: even in our weakest moments, God never leaves us. He meets us in our pain, giving us the strength to endure, the grace to persevere, and the hope of ultimate victory.

This chapter will dive into the spiritual reality of suffering—the battle for our souls. We'll explore how trials refine us, how perseverance can overcome the enemy's lies, and how God can redeem even our deepest pain for His glory. Suffering isn't easy, but with God's strength, it can transform us into something new.

Suffering Is A Battleground

When we face suffering, it's natural to wonder where

it's coming from. Is the Enemy behind this? Is he orchestrating my pain? While Scripture does reveal that Satan is often the cause of suffering—just look at Job's story or Paul's thorn in the flesh (2 Corinthians 12:7)—focusing too much on him can distract us from the real battle.

Here's the thing: the Enemy is going to do what the Enemy does. He comes to steal, kill, and destroy (John 10:10). That's his playbook. He wants to sow despair, doubt, and division in the midst of your pain. But your assignment in suffering isn't just about rebuking him—it's about resisting him. James 4:7 puts it plainly: "Resist the devil, and he will flee from you." Resisting isn't glamorous, but it's powerful. It's standing firm when everything in you wants to give up. It's holding on to God's promises even when the Enemy whispers lies. It's staying faithful when faith feels like the hardest thing to muster.

Sometimes, resisting the Enemy means telling him where he can go. Jesus modeled this in the wilderness when Satan came at Him with lies and temptations. With every attack, Jesus countered with Scripture, saying, "It is written" (Matthew 4:4-10). His authority over the Enemy came not from flashy declarations but from His unwavering obedience to God. And when Jesus stood firm, Satan had no choice but to leave.

But more often than not, the assignment in suffering isn't about engaging in spiritual smack talk. The real battle is about remaining faithful. It's about refusing to let the Enemy use your pain to derail your walk with God. That's true warfare. It's not just about what you say to the devil—it's about how you live in the midst of the struggle.

Faithfulness is your greatest weapon. Every moment you choose to trust God, worship Him through tears, and cling to His Word when life feels like it's falling apart—that's a victory over the Enemy.

Paul understood this kind of warfare. When he wrote to the Ephesians about putting on the full armor of God, his repeated instruction was to "stand" (Ephesians 6:13-14). Not charge into battle. Not defeat the Enemy single-handedly. Just stand.

Stand in the truth of who God is. Stand in the righteousness that comes through Christ. Stand in the gospel of peace, the shield of faith, and the hope of salvation.

Remember that your ability to stand firm in suffering makes the Enemy tremble because it's proof that his attacks can't separate you from God's love (Romans 8:38-39).

The real assignment in suffering isn't flashy, but it's holy. It's about letting your faith shine through the cracks. It's about declaring with your life that no amount of pain, no scheme of the devil, can pull you from the hands of your Savior. That's the kind of warfare that defeats the Enemy and glorifies God. So yes, tell the devil where he can go, but then fix your eyes on Jesus, the author and perfecter of your faith (Hebrews 12:2). In the end, faithfulness will always be your greatest victory.

The Enemy's Strategy

The enemy loves to use pain as a tool to sow doubt and despair. He whispers lies like, *You're too weak to handle this. God has abandoned you. There's no point in stay-*

ing. Just give up.

But here's the thing: Satan has no new tricks. He used the same strategies on Jesus in the wilderness—testing, twisting the truth, and trying to weaken His resolve (Matthew 4:1-11). If the enemy went after Jesus, he'll come after us, too. But Jesus didn't cave. He fought back with the Word of God, declaring truth in the face of temptation. And that's our weapon, too. When suffering threatens to crush us, we cling to the promises of Scripture: "God is our refuge and strength, an ever-present help in trouble" (Psalm 46:1).

Suffering can tempt us to slip into a victim mentality—a mindset that says, *This always happens to me,* or *I'll never get out of this.* It's a subtle trap, but it can steal our perspective and blind us to who we are as God's children. When we begin to see ourselves as helpless victims, we start to believe the lie that we are defined by our pain rather than by the God who calls us His own.

The Apostle Paul faced more suffering than most of us can imagine—beatings, shipwrecks, imprisonments, and constant danger (2 Corinthians 11:23-27). Yet, he never let his circumstances define his identity. Instead, he declared, "We are hard pressed on every side, but not crushed; perplexed, but not in despair; persecuted, but not abandoned; struck down, but not destroyed" (2 Corinthians 4:8-9). Paul refused to let his trials eclipse the truth of who he was in Christ.

When we embrace a victim mentality, we lose sight of God's sovereignty and His ability to redeem even the hardest seasons of our lives. It narrows our vision, making

213

it difficult to see the ways He's working in and through our pain.

But when we step back and remember our identity as beloved children of God, we reclaim the hope and strength He offers. We are not victims—we are victors through Christ (Romans 8:37). And though suffering is real, it doesn't define us. God does. Our pain may shape our journey, but it doesn't have the final word.

Outlasting The Enemy

Someone once said, "We defeat the devil when we simply outlast him." There's something gritty and hopeful in that thought—an invitation to stay the course even when it feels impossible. I love the idea that the most spiritual thing I can do in the midst of a battle is just to keep going. Not sprinting, not pretending everything is fine, but taking the next step, even if I feel like I'm crawling forward. It's not about ignoring the pain or faking strength—it's about holding on and trusting that God is holding on to me, too.

James 1:2-4 reminds us:

> *Consider it pure joy, my brothers and sisters, whenever you face trials of many kinds, because you know that the testing of your faith produces perseverance. Let perseverance finish its work so that you may be mature and complete, not lacking anything.*

That kind of joy doesn't mean plastering on a smile or being thankful for the suffering itself. It's about choosing to trust that the suffering has a purpose. It's about believing that God is working in the pain, even when we can't see it yet.

When we hold on, even by the skin of our teeth, we're letting perseverance do its work. It's not glamorous, and it's certainly not easy, but it's sacred. Every moment we stay in the fight, we're becoming more of who God has called us to be. Every step we take, no matter how small, strengthens the foundation of our faith.

Here's the thing: the devil doesn't play fair. He wants us to give up. He wants us to believe the lie that our suffering is meaningless or that God has abandoned us. But holding on is an act of defiance against those lies. It's a declaration that says, "I may be tired, I may be broken, but I'm not out."

In the book *Jesus Tempted in the Wilderness*, 19th-century preacher Adolphe Monod offers powerful encouragement for our spiritual battles:

> *Take courage. Stand firm. Do not shrink back a single step. Do not delay for a single instant. Leave the enemy no illusion. Show him that he is wasting his time and effort with you. Through the welcome you give him, force him to recognize within the disciple the Master who defeated him in the wilderness.*

Settle in your heart to become a problem to the Enemy—a stubborn, immovable thorn in his side. Be the kind of person who, every time your feet hit the floor in the morning, makes hell groan, "Oh no, not them again." Refuse to back down, give up, or go quietly. Let your prayers, faith, and obedience wreak havoc on his plans. Be a holy nuisance—a relentless reminder that he's already lost.

But more importantly, just be faithful and keep holding on! And as you hold on, know that you're not just enduring—you're growing. Perseverance isn't about surviving by sheer willpower; it's about partnering with God in the transformation process. It's about letting Him mold you into a person who is mature, complete, and deeply rooted in His love and purpose. And that, my friend, is worth the fight.

The Gold Refined In Fire

Have you ever paused to watch a blacksmith at work? It's fascinating, and honestly, it's a little intense—the fire roars, heating the metal until it's glowing red. Then come the hammer blows—loud, precise, and unrelenting. The sparks fly with every strike, and slowly but surely, something beautiful and purposeful emerges from what was once a misshapen hunk of metal. What looks like destruction is actually transformation.

This is exactly how suffering works in our faith. It doesn't feel good—far from it. The flames of hardship burn away at the things we rely on that aren't of God. The hammering trials shape us, even when it feels unbearable. Peter describes this process in vivid terms:

> *These [trials] have come so that the proven genuineness of your faith—of greater worth than gold—may result in praise, glory, and honor when Jesus Christ is revealed.*

| 1 Peter 1:7 NIV

Think about what Peter is saying here. Gold, one of the most valuable substances on Earth, has to go through fire to be purified. The impurities in raw gold can only be removed through intense heat—a process that melts and refines it, making it pure and even more valuable. Your faith, Peter says, is even more precious than gold. And it's through trials, through the fire of suffering, that it is refined and proven genuine.

This refining process isn't just about enduring for endurance's sake. It's about transformation. It's about God molding us into the people He created us to be. The things we thought we couldn't live without—the comforts, the plans, the securities—get stripped away in the fire, leaving behind something stronger, purer, and more reliant on Him.

Refining doesn't happen overnight. It's hot, intense, and painful. But the result? Faith that can stand firm. Faith that isn't shaken by every storm that comes its way. Faith that knows, even in the darkest valleys, that God is present and trustworthy.

When you're in the fire, it's easy to wonder if it will ever end. The heat feels unbearable, and the hammer strikes seem relentless. But remember this: the blacksmith doesn't put the metal in the fire to destroy it. He puts it there to transform it. He knows exactly how much heat it can take and how many blows are needed to achieve perfection.

God is the ultimate blacksmith. He knows the exact

temperature and pressure that will refine you without breaking you. The process may feel like it's too much, but He's there every step of the way, shaping you into someone who reflects His glory. Faith that has been through the fire becomes faith that's unshakable, a testimony to God's sustaining power and goodness. You may not understand it now, but one day, you'll see the beauty that came from the fire.

What Grows In The Valley

There's something interesting about mountaintops: nothing grows there. The view is incredible, and the air is crisp and clean, but the ground? It's barren. Growth doesn't happen on the mountaintop. It happens in the valley.

The valleys of life are where the soil is richest, and the same is true for our spiritual lives. Our faith takes root and grows in the valley—the seasons of suffering, loss, and struggle. The mountaintop moments, those high points where everything feels perfect and clear, are wonderful. But the real growth happens in the valleys, where we're forced to dig deep and rely on God in ways we never had before.

The valley strips us of our self-reliance. It exposes our limits and forces us to confront the fact that we can't do this on our own. And that's exactly where God wants us—not because He wants to see us suffer, but because He wants to show us His all-sufficient grace. It's in the valley that we learn His power is made perfect in our weakness. There, we find that His presence is enough to sustain us even when everything else is falling apart.

Think about the things that grow in a literal valley: lush vegetation, streams of water, thriving ecosystems. The valley is full of life, even though it's often shadowed by towering mountains on either side. Spiritually, the valley is where the most profound growth happens. It's where we discover that God is our refuge and strength, a very present help in trouble (Psalm 46:1). It's where we learn to trust Him, not just for the mountaintops but for the journey through the darkest places.

Faith isn't forged in the easy seasons. It's not built in times of comfort or ease. Faith is forged when you're at the end of yourself and life feels like it's crumbling around you, and you choose to hold on anyway. That's where God meets us, in the valley, and does His best work. He takes the broken pieces of our lives and creates something beautiful.

The valley may feel endless at times, but it has a purpose. It's not just a place of suffering—it's a place of transformation. The things God grows in the valley are things that couldn't take root anywhere else. And when you emerge, you'll see that even in the depths, God was with you, nurturing your faith, strengthening your soul, and preparing you for the next leg of the journey.

The battle in the valley is real, but the victory? That's worth every step.

Perpetua And Felicity: Faithful To The End

In the early days of Christianity, persecution was a constant threat. Yet, out of that suffering emerged stories of remarkable courage and faith. One of the most moving accounts is that of Perpetua and Felicity, two young women who remained faithful to Christ even as they faced brutal martyrdom. Perpetua, a 22-year-old noblewoman, was a new mother when she was arrested for her faith in Carthage around AD 203. Felicity, her servant, was visibly pregnant at the time of their imprisonment. Together with a group of fellow Christians, they were condemned to die in the arena for refusing to renounce their faith.

Perpetua's diary, written from her prison cell, gives us a rare glimpse into her courage and steadfastness. Despite her father's desperate pleas to deny Christ and save her life, Perpetua stood firm. "I cannot call myself by any other name than what I am—a Christian," she declared. Her words reflect a heart fully committed to God, even in the face of unimaginable suffering. Felicity, meanwhile, gave birth to her child while in prison. The thought of leaving her newborn behind was heart-wrenching, but her faith did not waver. "Now I am in the flesh, but I will not remain in the flesh," she reportedly said, expressing her hope in the resurrection.

On the day of their execution, Perpetua and Felicity were led into the arena, where they were subjected to brutal attacks by wild animals before being killed by the sword. Witnesses noted their calm resolve, even as they faced death. They prayed, encouraged one another, and walked into eternity with unwavering faith.

Their suffering was not meaningless; it was a testimony to the strength of their faith and the power of God to sustain His people in the darkest moments. The faith and courage of Perpetua and Felicity continue to inspire believers to this day, reminding us that no suffering—however great—can separate us from the love of God or diminish the hope of eternity. Their story challenges us to live with that same boldness, trusting that God is with us, even to the end.

Dietrich Bonhoeffer: Courage In The Face Of Evil

Few stories of faith in the face of suffering are as powerful as that of Dietrich Bonhoeffer, the German theologian and pastor who stood against the Nazi regime during World War II. Bonhoeffer's unwavering commitment to Christ and his courage in opposing Hitler's oppression ultimately led to his imprisonment and execution. His life and writings, particularly The Cost of Discipleship, remain a testament to enduring suffering with hope and courage.

Bonhoeffer wasn't content to sit on the sidelines as the Third Reich carried out its atrocities. He believed that true discipleship demanded action. In his resistance, Bonhoeffer joined the Confessing Church, a group that stood against the Nazi's co-opting of German Christianity. Later, he became involved in a plot to assassinate Hitler—a decision born from his conviction that faith without works was dead.

When Bonhoeffer was arrested in 1943, he faced the full weight of Nazi cruelty. Imprisoned for nearly two years, he endured harsh conditions and isolation. Yet, Bonhoeffer's faith remained unshaken even in the darkness of a prison cell. Letters smuggled from his cell reveal a man who, though grieved and physically weakened, refused to give in to despair. He famously wrote, "God does not give us everything we want, but He does fulfill His promises."

On April 9, 1945, just weeks before the end of the war, Bonhoeffer was executed by hanging at Flossenbürg concentration camp. Witnesses later recounted his calm demeanor and the peace with which he faced death, praying and trusting in God to the very end. His steadfast belief in the sovereignty of God shines through in his final recorded words: "This is the end—for me, the beginning of life."

Bonhoeffer's story is a profound reminder that suffering is often the battleground for deep spiritual growth. In the crucible of persecution, his faith was refined like gold. He faced evil with courage and endured suffering with the unshakable belief that God's purposes would ultimately prevail. As Winston Churchill put it, "We shall draw from the heart of suffering itself the means of inspiration and survival." Bonhoeffer's legacy inspires us to stand firm, even when the cost is great, trusting in the God who is sovereign over all.

Victory In Suffering

Suffering is the battlefield where faith is tested, the front lines where we wrestle with doubt, fear, and the enemy's relentless attacks. The enemy seeks to use pain as a weapon to weaken our resolve, but steadfast faith turns the tables, transforming suffering into a spiritual triumph. Scripture is filled with stories of warriors who endured suffering and came out victorious through their unwavering trust in God.

History gives us countless examples of believers who turned their pain into victory. Corrie ten Boom, imprisoned in a Nazi concentration camp, described God's sustaining power in her darkest hours: "There is no pit so deep, that God's love is not deeper still." In the face of unimaginable evil, her faith became a shield and her hope a weapon against despair. Like a seasoned soldier, she refused to let the enemy's tactics break her spirit. Her story reminds us that even in dire circumstances, God equips His children to stand firm.

When we endure suffering with faith, we're not just surviving—we're pushing back the darkness. Every time we choose to trust God in the middle of pain, we wield a spiritual weapon against the enemy's schemes. As warriors in the Kingdom, suffering becomes our battlefield, and our faith becomes the victory that overcomes the world.

Suffering has a way of reorienting us, of forcing us to see the battlefield of life with clearer eyes. It strips away the illusion of control and reminds us that our ultimate hope lies not in the fleeting comforts of this world but in the eternal promises of God. The Apostle Paul frames it like this: "For our light and momentary troubles are achieving for us an eternal glory that far outweighs them all. So we fix our eyes not on what is seen, but on what is unseen" (2 Corinthians 4:17-18). Paul knew that the trials of this life are temporary skirmishes in a war that has already been won.

Suffering sharpens our focus. It's like a soldier on the

battlefield, forced to shed unnecessary weight to run toward the fight. Grief, loss, and hardship may feel unbearable in the moment, but they can also reveal what really matters. They strip us down to the essentials—faith, hope, love—and remind us where our strength comes from. Suffering isn't just a burden to bear—it's often a wake-up call, reminding us to look beyond the fog of the battle to the Commander who leads us. There is something greater than the battle we're fighting and One who is fighting for us! Suffering, then, becomes not just a battlefield but a proving ground. It's where our faith is refined, our endurance is strengthened, and our hope is set on the eternal Kingdom.

The Warrior's Reward

Suffering calls us into the fight—a battle for faith, endurance, and trust in the midst of pain. It's not a skirmish to avoid but a holy war where God's strength is made perfect in our weakness. The fight may leave scars, but those scars tell the story of a faith that didn't back down, a hope that wasn't extinguished, and a God who never abandoned His soldiers.

Paul understood this fight well: "I have fought the good fight, I have finished the race, I have kept the faith. Now there is in store for me the crown of righteousness" (2 Timothy 4:7-8). For the warrior of faith, suffering is not the end—it's a pathway to glory, a road that leads to a victory far greater than we can imagine. The enemy's attacks, no matter how relentless, are no match for the power of a steadfast faith anchored in Christ.

Take a moment to pause and reflect with this prayer:

> *Lord, I don't understand all the battles I face, but I trust You as my Commander and shield. Give me the strength to fight, the courage to endure, and the faith to see beyond the pain. Thank You for the victory You have already won for me through Christ. Lead me onward, and may Your glory shine through my struggles. Amen.*

In the heat of the battle, remember this: **you're not fighting alone**. The Commander of Heaven's armies stands with you, and the victory is already secure. Stand firm, soldier. The warrior's reward is worth every trial.

Trish's Story

My worldview was shaped by a kind of Christianity that put too much emphasis on the appearance of righteousness. I was taught, or maybe just absorbed, that God is always evaluating our performance, and we either please or displease Him with every thought, word, and action. I always compared myself to others to see if I measured up, and of course, I never did. The deepest desire of my heart was for God to love me, and what I believed with my whole heart was that He only did when I was good enough.

This belief informed every aspect of my life growing up and into my marriage. My husband Ben and I had both come from broken families, and we were determined to stay together no matter what. We quickly had three unique, smart boys, and I threw myself into motherhood.

I began homeschooling them, relishing the chance to learn together and grow strong relationships as a family. Even as I trained up my children in the Lord, my conviction that I wasn't fully accepted and loved by God remained.

Then came Kate. Our fourth and final child was a girl who changed my relationship with God forever. Watching her grow up, I was fascinated by the way she was so free to just be herself. I kept waiting for her to start comparing herself to others, but she never did.

She seemed so confident and comfortable. She had a sweet, playful relationship with her Dad, and it filled my heart to see them together. She and I had so many great conversations as we did school together, and when she was five, she gave her heart to Jesus and was baptized. Her faith was so sweet and innocent that it made me truly face my battle with God over whether He loved me unconditionally or not. I decided that I could not fight God and win; if He says He loves me, He does. I did not feel like He loved me, but I had conceded the fight and, as an act of my will, decided to accept that He did.

Kate grew, and our relationship grew, too. I didn't take it for granted. I knew that most moms have difficult seasons with their daughters, but Kate was just… kind. I was getting to witness what it is like growing up knowing you're loved no matter what. I was excited to see her in her teenage years and then as a young woman. She was my future friend, and I couldn't wait to see what God would do with her life. She was passionate about dance and spent her days practicing her choreography and studying the videos of older dancers at her studio.

Then, on April 7th, 2018, our world turned upside down. I was getting her ready for dance pictures when she collapsed in my arms. Ben and I took her to Urgent Care, and they sent us straight to the ER. After several tests, we heard the words no parent should ever hear:

"Your child has leukemia."

We wouldn't be going home; we would be admitted to the hospital to start treatment. At that moment, God dropped a word for Kate into my heart-adventure. Adventures are sometimes scary, but we were going to meet new people, we were going to learn new things, and we were going to depend on God more than ever. We were going to be in this together as a family.

I discussed this with Kate when the doctor left the room, and she was instantly the bravest girl I'd ever seen. She wasn't afraid, and she didn't ask why. She just told her Dad to remember to bring her stuffed panda when he went home to pack her bag. She was nine years old.

The doctors did not waste time. Kate immediately had a blood transfusion. What was this new world we were living in? Some stranger's blood was helping my daughter. That night was a sleepless one for me as I realized that Kate was now a child like the ones on those St. Jude commercials, the ones with no hair (her curls!) and a tube going into their nose. Was that what was in store for her?

I knew nothing about cancer, but I was now a "Cancer Mom." The official name for her disease was Pre-B Acute Lymphoblastic Leukemia. Everyone said that if you have to get a cancer, this is the one you wanted. This treatment protocol had been established for her type of cancer decades ago and had a 90% survival rate. My breathing began to relax a tiny bit with this clear path forward and the high probability for Kate to get through this.

One morning that first week, I was listening to the day's Bible reading from Acts 5:40-41:

> *They called in the apostles and had them flogged. Then they ordered them never again to speak the name of Jesus, and they let them go. The apostles left the high council rejoicing that God had counted them worthy to suffer disgrace for the name of Jesus.*

And right then, everything became quiet in my mind except His whisper: "That's you (and Kate). I've counted you worthy to suffer this for my name." In my life, I had felt the shame of rejection, believing the lie that He didn't love me and that I wasn't one of the chosen ones. But with that word, this utter certainty that He was with us in this suffering filled my heart. This was so much bigger than I could see. He had chosen us for this task. I could not wait to praise Him at the big party we would throw to celebrate how God healed Kate of cancer.

But that's not what happened.
Not at all.

After only twelve days of cancer treatment, Kate got a bacterial infection, and with her immune system annihilated by chemotherapy, her body went into septic shock. Kate threw up blood. Lots of it. For two hours, I wiped it off her mouth and chin until she told me it hurt. I let the blood leak out and down her neck, onto her shirt. Her final words were, "When can I go to sleep?" She was so tired. They sedated her, and her eyes closed. My feet led me to the bathroom to wash my precious daughter's blood off my hands and arms. An unknown sound came up from some-where- was that me? Was I crying, screaming, gasping? Her blood washed into the sink. Ben and I were guided into a private waiting room, and once the door shut behind me, I began to cry, "I need her. I need her. I need her." I wept until I could feel nothing but a hole in my chest and an ache in my head. This was my worst nightmare.

She stayed ventilated and sedated in the Pediatric Intensive Care Unit for seven long days and nights. And this is where I must tell you some things that might not make sense. That hospital room became a holy place. Ask anyone who was there. God was in the room.

As I watched the effects of massive infection destroy my daughter's body, I felt His strong arms around me. I looked at Kate and was stricken with love for her. All I wanted was to be with her. She was more precious than anything to me. And that's when I heard His voice again: "This is how I feel about you. This is how I feel about all my children."

In that instant, fear left. I knew His love for me was real. I could feel it. It's more than I can comprehend.

Kate went to heaven on April 26. Her adventure had started just twenty days before. During that time, she had written in her prayer journal once. Her words are etched on my heart, and I quote them often.

She wrote:

> *Even in the hard and hurting, You are still my Father. I praise You even when I'm weak, and I thank You for everything You've done to me, and I ask You not only to heal me but everyone who needs it. Amen.*

Kate completed her mission on Earth in just over nine years. Some of us take longer. After she went to heaven, my mind was continually there. I would wake up and say to myself, "Well, ok, I woke up here. He must have something important in eternity for me to do today because He knows I'd rather be with Kate in heaven." I'd ask Jesus to help me make a difference with His love that day. It was my way of fighting for joy in the midst of the gut-wrenching pain of missing Kate. I would not let my daughter's mission end without making the biggest impact it could.

I now call Kate my partner beyond the veil. I have witnessed so many amazing things happen through her story and the legacy she left. I refuse to let the enemy get any victory from this tragedy, and I take every chance I get to tell of God's immeasurable love for us. My goal is to gather as many people as possible for the party we will surely have in heaven one day- the one where we praise God for all the good He did through one girl's life and, yes, how He healed her from cancer.

God's love is now my solid foundation. His story for us is for our eternal life to be the best it can be, and all our suffering here is temporary. My nine years with Kate are just the first nine of infinity. My hope is not in this world anymore; it's in heaven with Jesus, and He is all I need.

CHAPTER EIGHT

HOPE IN SUFFERING

The words of Jesus in John 16:33 encapsulate the tension we all feel: "In this world you will have trouble. But take heart! I have overcome the world." Trouble, trials, and suffering are guaranteed, but so is the hope that Christ has already secured victory over it all.

Hope is not an escape from suffering—it's the steady assurance that even in the fire, God is with us, working all things for good. It's the vision of an eternal glory that far outweighs the heaviest pain (2 Corinthians 4:17). It's knowing that your story doesn't end in darkness because Christ's story didn't end in the tomb.

I want to invite you to step into hope, even when it feels risky. It's a call to lean into the promises of God, who not only walks with you through suffering but also redeems it.

Hope In The Dark

St. Teresa of Ávila, the 16th-century Spanish mystic and Carmelite reformer, lived a life marked by deep suffering. Her reflections on pain and perseverance have become a source of hope for generations. One of her most well-known sayings encapsulates her eternal perspective: "In light of heaven, the worst suffering on earth will be seen to be no more serious than one night in an inconvenient hotel." This vivid and even comedic metaphor challenges believers to view their trials through the lens of eternity, a perspective Teresa herself lived out through profound hardship.

From chronic illnesses that left her debilitated for years to the immense resistance she faced while reforming the Carmelite order, Teresa's journey of faith was anything but smooth. Yet, perhaps her greatest struggle came in what she described as the "dark night of the soul," a term later popularized by her fellow mystic, St. John of the Cross. For nearly 50 years, Teresa wrestled with an aching sense of God's absence. 50 years! Her prayers often felt dry, her soul parched, and her connection to the divine distant and elusive. And yet, in the midst of this spiritual desolation, she clung to God with unwavering resolve.

This prolonged season of struggle taught Teresa that hope isn't the absence of hardship or doubt—it's choosing to trust God in the silence. Reflecting on this hard-won truth, she wrote,

> *Let nothing disturb you, let nothing frighten you, all things are passing away; God never changes.*

These words weren't just poetic; they were a declaration of faith shaped by years of enduring pain and perseverance in trust.

She endured significant physical suffering, including a severe illness that left her paralyzed for several years. Even in her weakness, Teresa found strength in knowing God was with her. She once remarked, "Pain is never permanent." For Teresa, suffering was not something to be feared but an opportunity to grow closer to God and refine her character. Her writings, particularly *The Interior Castle* and *The Way of Perfection*, reflect a deep understanding of the soul's journey toward God, emphasizing surrender, perseverance, and trust, even in the darkest moments.

Teresa's reflections on suffering consistently pointed toward eternity. For her, the trials of life were temporary, but the joy of heaven was everlasting. She encouraged others to hold onto this perspective, writing, "The soul, if it is truly resigned, need fear nothing. It fears neither trials nor suffering, because it sees that these make it pleasing to God." Her words challenge us to lift our eyes beyond the pain of the present moment and see the refining work of God in our lives.

St. Teresa's life speaks powerfully to those in their own dark nights, whether spiritual, physical, or emotional. Her unwavering hope is a call to persevere, to trust that God is at work even when He feels far away, and to cling to the truth that every trial, no matter how daunting, is temporary.

Offensive Hope

Hope can feel offensive because it demands that we hold two seemingly opposite realities in tension: the pain of our present and the promise of our future. It doesn't ask us to choose one over the other. Instead, it allows us to fully acknowledge our pain while still believing in God's promise to make all things new.

In the thick of suffering, hope can feel risky, even dangerous. To hope is to open yourself to the possibility of disappointment. Have you ever felt that tension? It's much easier to harden your heart and lower your expectations. But biblical hope doesn't hinge on outcomes we can control—it's anchored in God's unchanging character and His promises.

During my cancer journey, there were moments when the weight of it all made me want to shut out any notion of hope. People would encourage me to "hold on," and I'd think, You don't understand what this feels like. I wasn't mad at them; I just couldn't connect with their optimism.

But here's the thing about hope: it doesn't depend on how you feel in the moment. It's not about summoning up the right emotions or faking positivity. Hope is stubborn. It anchors us to God's promises, even when our circumstances try to drag us under.

One day stands out to me vividly. I was wrestling with God, asking all the questions we ask when life feels like too much. "Why me? Why this? Where are You in this pain?" There were no immediate answers. But in that raw, vulnerable space, Holy Spirit reminded me of the words of Christ in John 15:15:

> *I am the vine; you are the branches. If you remain in me and I in you, you will bear much fruit; apart from me, you can do nothing.*

For the first time, I saw my cancer diagnosis as something other than a curse. It was an opportunity—a rare and incredibly precious invitation to abide.

To abide means to remain, to dwell, to be rooted. It's not about striving harder or doing more; it's about staying connected to the source of life. In his classic work Abide in Christ, Andrew Murray writes:

> *The connection between the vine and the branch is a living one. The branch does not only come to the vine for its sap, but it lives in the vine and depends on it entirely for all it needs to bear fruit.*

When we abide in Christ, we are reminded that our strength is not our own. Life's storms may bend us, but they cannot break us if we are rooted in Him. Abiding means we draw from His life, not our limited reserves. In this dependence, we find the grace to endure suffering and the strength to bear fruit even in the hardest seasons.

In his book, *The Practice of the Presence of God*, Brother Lawrence emphasizes the simplicity and necessity of staying connected to Christ throughout our daily lives. He writes, "We ought not to be weary of doing little things for the love of God, who regards not the greatness of the work but the love with which it is performed." This continual abiding transforms even the mundane into something sacred, reminding us that Christ is present and sufficient in every moment.

Abiding doesn't mean life will be free of hardship. In fact, it often means the opposite. Jesus reminds us in John 15:2 that the Father prunes the branches so they can bear more fruit. Pruning is painful, but it's also purposeful. It's through abiding in Christ that we can trust the process, knowing that even in seasons of loss or trial, God is shaping us into His image.

This is the essence of hope: it's not the absence of grief but the presence of faith.

It's clinging to the belief that God's promises outweigh our present pain. Hope isn't about denying the pain.

It's about declaring: *This is not the end of the story.*

It's about trusting that the God who stood with Shadrach, Meshach, and Abednego in the fire, the God who bore the cross for the joy set before Him, is the same God who holds us steady in our darkest moments.

During those six months of chemotherapy treatments, I learned the true meaning of abiding. Sometimes, I could do nothing else but simply abide. To know that He was with me, that He held me, that I was in Him. And that gave me hope.

If hope feels offensive to you right now, you're not alone. You don't have to summon it up on your own. Lean into God's promises, even when your faith feels shaky. Let His Word remind you that the story isn't over. He's still writing a masterpiece with your life, and though the chapter you're in may be dark, the ending is one of glory, joy, and redemption.

The True Nature Of Hope

"Well, I hope so!" This common refrain of a doubting mind is often what we think about when we reflect on the word hope. But hope is not wishful thinking. Hope is not blind optimism. It's not a vague wish that everything will work out or a superficial positivity that denies the reality of suffering.

Hope doesn't wave away the complexity of grief or minimize the pain of life's most profound losses. Hope is also not an escape. It doesn't mean ignoring the hard questions, pushing down the grief, or pretending everything is okay. True hope confronts pain head-on. It acknowledges the weight of what's been lost, the brokenness of the world, and the real toll suffering takes on the human spirit. Hope doesn't deny the valley; it chooses to walk through it, holding on to something greater.

Biblical hope is far deeper than mere wishful thinking. It's enduring, unshakable, and anchored not in circumstances but in the character and promises of God. The writer of Hebrews describes it as "an anchor for the soul, firm and secure"(Hebrews 6:19). Just as a ship's anchor holds it steady against the push and pull of the waves, hope rooted in Christ holds us steady when life's storms threaten to overwhelm us.

One of the clearest explanations of hope comes from Paul in Romans 5:3-5:

> *We also glory in our sufferings, because we know that suffering produces perseverance; perseverance, charac-*

ter; and character, hope. And hope does not put us to shame, because God's love has been poured out into our hearts through the Holy Spirit, who has been given to us.

Notice the progression—hope doesn't spring up overnight. It's a process born from suffering and forged through perseverance. Hope is the hard-won fruit of faith tested and proven in the fires of life's trials.

This hope is not wishful thinking or naïve optimism. It's the assurance that God is at work even in the face of uncertainty. As believers, we are invited to trust in the promises of a God who is good, faithful, and sovereign. This kind of hope doesn't minimize pain but points us to the larger story—the story of a God who redeems, restores, and makes all things new (Revelation 21:5).

"Hope is the confident assurance that good is on the way."

This phrase captures the essence of biblical hope. It's not rooted in the idea that our circumstances will instantly improve or that we'll avoid hardship altogether. Instead, it's rooted in the unchanging truth that God is working all things for good for those who love Him (Romans 8:28). This doesn't mean the pain will always make sense in the moment, but it does mean that no suffering is wasted. God, in His infinite wisdom, weaves even the darkest threads of our lives into His redemptive tapestry.

God Isn't Looking For Heroes

It was one of those days—the kind that stopped me in

my tracks and left me gasping for air. The kind of news that brought me to my knees, where life felt unbearable, and the weight of grief pressed down with unrelenting force. It shook me to my core.

The bad news didn't stop coming. For weeks and months to come, the problems seemed to ramp up. If it wasn't so painful, it would be humorous. It was one of the most challenging seasons of life I've walked through. I wrestled with God in ways I never had before. After everything I had given for Him, after all the sacrifices I thought I'd made, I found myself angry, heartbroken, and utterly undone.

My view of God—and myself—was turned upside down. The foundations I'd built my faith on felt cracked, like they might crumble beneath me. In that raw and broken state, I wept before Him. I didn't hold back. I told Him everything—how hopeless I felt, how much this pain was too heavy for me to bear. My grief laid me bare, and with it came the humbling realization that the "superhero Christianity" I'd clung to, the idea that I should be able to handle anything, that my "important assignment" from God would keep me and my family immune from real suffering, it all was a lie. All of it.

I spent a long time sitting with my grief, bringing it before the Lord in the only way I knew how. I also sat with a counselor, giving voice to the pain I'd kept bottled up inside, slowly untangling the knots of sorrow and confusion. Although my experience wasn't that of Job's—his losses and trials were far beyond anything I've ever faced—I understood how he must have felt on some level. The ache of unanswered questions, the weight of suffering that seemed too heavy to bear, the deep confusion about why God would allow such pain—all of it resonated with me.

I hadn't lost everything like Job, but I wrestled with the same bewildering questions: "Why, God? Why now? Why this?" In those moments, Job's story didn't feel like ancient history; it felt raw and present, like I was living a shadow of his struggle in my own way. Though our circumstances were worlds apart, the thread of shared humanity—the vulnerability, the pain, and the desperate longing for God to make sense of it all—connected me to him.

So, in my own version of sackcloth and ashes, I sat down, stripped of every pretense, and began to write:

> *Sitting in the rubble and ruin of failure, dreams dashed on the rocks, and painfully unmet expectations, these children of God are no less children.*
>
> *They've been through the fire and have come out on the other side unburned, yet exhausted from the extreme heat that has sapped them of strength. The fires of hell licked about them but could not touch them. And yet their sacrifices of praise are forced through parched lips.*
>
> *These who heard the call of God to lay down their lives and did so were once met with accolades from exuberant spectators, cheering on these "heroes" of the faith. Something of their praise made its way into their souls and convinced them of their heroism. And so, with unmatched zeal, they set out to change the world.*

And now, in the silence of isolation, heaping ashes on their heads, with the distant and faint blast of the bugles that summoned them to the grand arena of their purpose, the "heroes" wonder how they got here. As their names are swiftly forgotten by the adoring crowds, the dreams they carried seem to slip away as a memory as well. The world wasn't changed in an instant as they had hoped. Their bravery, as daring as it is, seems to have gotten them as far as the wilderness.

And in this desert, beneath the shade of the withering tree, they are reminded of this sobering yet liberating thought: God isn't looking for heroes.

Not heroes. Just the faithful. His eyes roam to and fro in search of the ones foolish enough to still be in the game when the outcome seems to be already called. People who keep trusting even when the silence is deafening. The praying sufferers. The joy-finders.
And when life hands them lemons, they don't bother making lemonade, turning bad into good. No. They just keep walking, resolute in their devotion to Him who makes good of all things in His time. There are finer things to be had than lemonade, because on this long, treacherous journey, He Himself has become their sustenance.

"Hero." The truly heroic are the ones who would never claim that title. They wouldn't dare share it with a real One. God isn't looking for heroes. He's looking for a humble company who've found Him to be theirs.

If you feel like you have to be the hero—the one who holds everything together, the strong one who never cracks, the unshakable rock in the middle of life's storms—let me gently remind you: that's not your job.

It's easy to fall into the trap of thinking that God expects you to keep it all together, to never falter, and to bear the weight of the world on your shoulders. But if life has fallen apart and you're still reeling from the shock of discovering that you're not bulletproof, hear this encouragement: you were never meant to be.

There's only one hero in your story, and His name is Jesus. He's the one who holds you together when everything else is crumbling. He's the one who carried the cross and bore the weight of sin and suffering so you wouldn't have to. He's not asking you to be invincible—He's inviting you to lean on Him when you feel like you can't take another step.

Being human means we're not supposed to have it all figured out or carry every burden on our own. It's okay to admit you're not strong enough, that you're scared, or that you don't have all the answers. It's ok to tell Him that you're feeling hopeless or lost. Jesus isn't disappointed in your weakness; He meets you there, offering His strength in exchange for your surrender. Let go of the myth that you have to be your own savior, and let Him be what only He can be—your hope, the anchor, the sustainer, and the true hero of your story.

Hope That Holds

Hope is a tension. It is the space between what we long

for and what we have, between what is promised and what is present. To walk with hope is to live in the paradox of the now and the not yet—trusting that God is at work here, in this moment, while also knowing that the fullness of His kingdom is still unfolding.

Many of us wrestle with hope because we've been disappointed before. We've prayed and waited, stood in faith, clung to promises—and yet, healing hasn't come, the breakthrough hasn't arrived, and the suffering hasn't lifted. So what do we do? Do we stop hoping to protect ourselves from future disappointment? Do we lower our expectations of God so that we aren't crushed when He doesn't move in the way we desperately desire? The answer isn't to hope less but to hope *differently*.

Hope was never meant to be a fragile thing. When it is tied too tightly to a specific outcome—God will heal me exactly like this, He will fix my situation exactly when I want Him to—hope can become brittle. It turns into something we clutch with white-knuckled fists, which fractures when reality does not align with our expectations.

But biblical hope is not a demand—it's a confidence in the One who holds all things, even when we don't understand how He is holding them. The kingdom of God is breaking into this world, yes, but it is also still coming in its fullness. That means we stand in the reality that God heals now, that miracles happen now, and that redemption is unfolding now—but we also know that we are not home yet. The full renewal of all things is still ahead.

This is where hope must be rightly rooted. Not in an outcome, but in a Person.

The Tension Of The Kingdom

When Jesus walked the earth, He declared, "The kingdom of God is at hand" (Mark 1:15). He healed the sick, raised the dead, and restored the broken. His very presence was evidence that God's reign was invading a world groaning under suffering. Yet, He also spoke of a future kingdom—a time when sorrow would be no more.

We live between these two realities. The kingdom is here, but it is also still coming. This is why we see glimpses of healing, but not always the full restoration we long for. It is why some prayers are miraculously answered while others seem to echo in silence. It is why we hold onto hope, but we hold it in a way that does not crumble when God's timeline differs from ours.

To hope well is to stand in this tension: believing fiercely that God can move now while also surrendering to the mystery when it doesn't look like what we imagined.

How Do We Walk This Out?

Pray boldly, but trust fully. Ask for healing. Ask for breakthrough. Ask with confidence, just as Jesus invited us to (John 14:13-14). But also surrender the results to Him. True faith is not just believing in miracles—it is trusting in God's goodness even when the miracle does not come in the way we expect.

Hold onto God's character, not just His works. Hope rooted in an outcome is shaky ground. But hope rooted in God's nature—His love, wisdom, and sovereignty—is unshakable. If our hope is only in what God does, we will struggle when He does not act in the way we want. But if our hope is in who He is, we can stand firm even in the waiting.

Live expectantly, without entitlement. There is a difference between expecting God to move and demanding how He must move. Faith invites us to lean in with expectation, believing that God is still working, that His power is still real, and that His kingdom is still advancing. But entitlement sneaks in when we start to believe that God owes us a specific outcome. Faith says, "I believe You will." Entitlement says, "You must." The former leads to hope; the latter leads to resentment.

Keep your eyes on eternity, without neglecting today. Some people despair because they put all their hope in the now, forgetting that ultimate healing is still ahead. Others detach from hope altogether, saying, "Well, one day in heaven, things will be better," while numbing themselves to pain in the present. Both miss the fullness of biblical hope. We are called to believe for God's power to move today, while knowing that ultimate restoration is still coming in eternity.

Romans 5:5 tells us that hope does not put us to shame because God's love has been poured into our hearts. This is not a flimsy hope—it is a durable one. It is a hope that withstands unanswered prayers. A hope that does not collapse under suffering. A hope that looks for miracles today but does not despair when we must wait for them.

Hold onto hope. But hold it rightly. Not in a timeline. Not in a perfect resolution. Not in a guaranteed outcome. Hold it in the person of Jesus—the One who heals, the One who saves, the One who walks with us now, and the One who will one day make all things new.

This is the tension we live in.
This is the hope that will not break.

An Invitation To Hope

As you reach this point in your journey, pause for a moment and reflect. Where have you seen glimpses of hope, even in the midst of your darkest days? What are the promises of God that you are clinging to right now? This is an invitation—not to pretend the pain doesn't exist, but to look for the hand of God working in the middle of it.

What would it look like to embrace this kind of hope today? Perhaps it starts with honest questions:

- Where in my life do I feel the weight of hopelessness the most?

- What lies about God or myself might I be believing in this season?

- How has God already shown His faithfulness, even in small ways?

- What scripture or promise of God can I cling to right now?

Sometimes, hope is found in small, deliberate steps.

Here are some practical ways to embrace hope, even when it feels far away:

Spend time in God's Word: Focus on passages that speak to His faithfulness, like Lamentations 3:22-23, Romans 8:28, or Isaiah 41:10. Write them down and read them daily.

Pray honestly: Tell God exactly how you're feeling—your doubts, fears, and frustrations. Then, ask Him to fill you with His hope.

Seek community: Share your struggles with trusted friends or mentors who can encourage you, pray for you, and remind you of truth when you need it most.

Keep a gratitude journal: Each day, write down one thing you're thankful for, even if it's small. Gratitude has a way of shifting our perspective.

Take care of yourself: Sometimes embracing hope starts with simple acts like resting, eating well, or spending time in creation to be reminded of God's handiwork.

Celebrate small victories: Even the smallest step forward is worth acknowledging. God works in the seemingly insignificant moments.

This kind of hope doesn't erase suffering, but it transforms it. It gives purpose to the pain, strength for the journey, and a vision of the eternal joy that lies ahead. Imagine the difference this hope could make in your life—not just as a coping mechanism but as a lifeline rooted in the unshakable promises of God.

So, here's the challenge: will you dare to hope? Will you trust that the God who holds the universe also holds your heart? Hope may not calm the storm instantly, but it will hold you steady until the skies clear. God is faithful, His promises are sure, and His love will never fail.

Step into this invitation to hope—not because life is easy, but because God is with you. And that changes everything.

The End Of Suffering

> *In that day the LORD with his hard and great and strong sword will punish Leviathan the fleeing serpent, Leviathan the twisting serpent, and he will slay the dragon that is in the sea.*

Isaiah 27:1 ESV

One of my favorite works of art is *Destruction of Leviathan* by Gustave Doré. In this 19th-century etching, the artist masterfully captures a moment of cosmic triumph. The image depicts God delivering the final blow to Leviathan, the mythical sea monster that represents chaos, evil, and rebellion against divine order in biblical and ancient Near Eastern thought. Leviathan thrashes in the waters, a once fearsome creature now subdued and defeated by the Creator's overwhelming power. There is a rawness to Doré's lines, a sense that the battle is both ancient and eternal, but the outcome is certain: chaos will not reign forever.

To the people of the ancient world, the waters weren't just a natural element—they represented a threat to order and life. The Bible, deeply aware of this imagery, speaks of God as the One who rules over the waters, bringing order out of chaos. The very opening verses of Genesis portray this: "Now the earth was formless and empty, darkness was over the surface of the deep, and the Spirit of God was hovering over the waters" (Genesis 1:2). God's first act of creation is to bring light, form, and boundaries to the chaotic void.

This imagery of taming the waters and defeating Leviathan recurs throughout Scripture. Job 41 describes Leviathan as an untamable beast, symbolizing forces beyond human control. Psalm 74 speaks of God crushing the heads of Leviathan and dividing the sea to make a path for His people (Psalm 74:13-14). God is always the One who holds the final authority.

In the New Testament, this theme is carried forward in profound ways. Jesus repeatedly demonstrates His authority over the chaos of the waters. In Mark 4:35-41, Jesus rebukes a violent storm, calming the sea with just His words: "Peace! Be still!" The disciples, awestruck, ask, "Who then is this, that even the wind and the sea obey Him?" (Mark 4:41). Here is more than a man—this is the God of Genesis, the One who hovers over the waters, stilling them with His command.

The ultimate defeat of chaos and evil comes through Jesus' death and resurrection. On the cross, He takes on the full force of sin, suffering, and death—the very essence of chaos. In His resurrection, He demonstrates His victory over them. Revelation brings this cosmic narrative to its conclusion. In Revelation 21:1, John writes, "Then I saw a new heaven and a new earth, for the first heaven and the first earth had passed away, and there was no longer any sea." This isn't about the physical absence of oceans but the eradication of chaos. The waters, once a symbol of disorder, are gone, replaced by the eternal order and peace of God's new creation.

Doré's *Destruction of Leviathan* is a visual echo of this biblical truth. In its dark, swirling lines, we see the remnants of chaos—a reminder of the struggles, pain, and rebellion plaguing the world. But at the center stands God, unyielding and victorious. The battle belongs to Him, and His victory is final.

The suffering and chaos we endure are real but not ultimate. Jesus, who drank the bitter cup of suffering on our behalf, is also the One who stilled the storm, walked on the waves, and will one day crush the head of Leviathan, eradicating every source of chaos and pain. His triumph ensures that one day, every tear will be wiped away, and the waters of chaos will be no more (Revelation 21:4).

So take heart.

The storm may rage, the Leviathan may thrash, the bitter cup may sting—but none of it will have the final word. Jesus does. He is the Alpha and the Omega, the One who drank suffering to its dregs so that we could taste eternal joy. The cross was real. The pain was real. But so was the resurrection.

And so is the promise: He is making all things new.

This is not wishful thinking. This is not fragile hope.

This is the unshakable truth of a Kingdom that cannot be shaken.

One day, the sea will be stilled, the serpent slain, and the bitter cup shattered. Until then, we hope—not because we are strong, but because He is. Not because we understand, but because we trust. And not because the suffering is over, but because the victory is already won.

Acknowledgments

Writing this book has been its own kind of journey—a mix of wrestling, learning, and discovering new depths of God's presence in the hard stuff. I'm deeply grateful to the people who walked with me through this process and shaped my thoughts.

To my therapist, Rachel Church: thank you for helping me untangle my own story and for reminding me that it's okay to sit with the hard questions. Your encouragement and insight have been invaluable, not just for this book, but for my life.

To Ashley, Dale, Daisy, Andrea, Collin, and Trish, who graciously let me include your personal stories in these pages: your vulnerability and courage in sharing your journeys through suffering have inspired me more than I can express. Your walk with God in the valley is nothing short of heroic. Thank you for trusting me with your sacred moments.

To my wife, Bethany: you are my constant, my biggest encourager, and the one who walks beside me in every season. Thank you for your love, your patience, and your steady belief in me.

To my friends and church family: your prayers, encouragement, and shared struggles have given this book a heartbeat. Your willingness to be real about faith and suffering has made me bolder in my own writing.

And finally, to you—the reader: thank you for picking up this book and allowing me to walk alongside you. My prayer is that these pages will remind you of the hope and presence of a God who doesn't shy away from our pain but meets us in the middle of it.

With all my gratitude,

Gunter

Bibliography

1. Epictetus. *Discourses*. Translated by Robin Hard. London: Everyman's Library, 1995.

2. Marcus Aurelius. *Meditations*. Translated by Gregory Hayes. New York: Modern Library, 2002.

3. Plato. *The Republic*. Translated by G.M.A. Grube, revised by C.D.C. Reeve. Indianapolis: Hackett Publishing Company, 1992.

4. Aristotle. *Nicomachean Ethics*. Translated by Terence Irwin. Indianapolis: Hackett Publishing Company, 1999.

5. Laozi. *Tao Te Ching*. Translated by D.C. Lau. New York: Penguin Classics, 1963.

6. Confucius. *The Analects*. Translated by Arthur Waley. New York: Vintage Books, 1989.

7. *The Bible: Job, Psalms, Philippians, Romans, Revelation*. English Standard Version. Wheaton, IL: Crossway Bibles, 2016.

8. Augustine. *City of God*. Translated by Henry Bettenson. New York: Penguin Classics, 2003.

9. Aquinas, Thomas. *Summa Theologica*. Translated by the Fathers of the English Dominican Province. Westminster, MD: Christian Classics, 1981.

10. Al-Ghazali. *The Revival of the Religious Sciences*. Translated by Nabih Amin Faris. Lahore: Sh. Muhammed Ashraf, 1962.

11. Hume. *Dialogues Concerning Natural Religion*. Edited by Richard H Popkin. Indianapolis: Hackett Publishing Company, 1980.

12. Voltaire. *Candide*. Translated by Theo Cuffe. New York: Penguin Classics, 2005.

13. Nietzsche, Friedrich. *Thus Spoke Zarathustra*. Translated by Walter Kauffman. New York: Modern Library, 1995.

14. University of Southampton. (n.d.). 1.3 *God and evil: Nietzsche*. https://www.southampton.ac.uk/philosophy/undergraduate/decision-trees/god-and-evil/1-3.page.

15. Sartre. *Being and Nothingness: An Essay in Phenomenological Ontology*. Translated by Hazel E. Barnes. New York: Washington Square Press, 1992.

16. Nussbaum, Martha C. *Upheavals of Thought: The Intelligence of Emotions*. Cambridge: Cambridge University Press, 2001.

17. *The Qur'an*. Transplanted by M.A.S. Abdel Haleem. Oxford: Oxford University Press, 2004. (Surah 2:155–157)

18. *The Bhagavad Gita*. Translated by Eknath Easwaran. Tomales, CA: Nilgiri Press, 2007.

19. *The Avesta: The Sacred Books of the Zoroastrian Religion*. Translated by James Darmesteter and L.H. Mills. Oxford: Clarendon Press, 1880-1887.

20. Neusner, Jacob. *Rabbinic Literature: An Essential Guide*. Abingdon Press, 2005.

21. Boyd, Gregory A. *God at War: The Bible and Spiritual Conflict*. InterVarsity Press, 1997.

22. Wink, Walter. *The Powers That Be: Theology for a New Millennium*. Doubleday, 1998.

23. Heiser, Michael S. *The Unseen Realm: Recovering the Supernatural Worldview of the Bible*. Lexham Press, 2015.

24. Longman III, Tremper, and Daniel G. Reid. *God Is a Warrior*. Zondervan, 1995.

25. Terrien, Samuel. *The Elusive Presence: Toward a New Biblical Theology*. Harper & Row, 1978.

26. Brueggemann, Walter. *The Prophetic Imagination*. Fortress Press, 1978.

27. Greenberg, Irving. *"Cloud of Smoke, Pillar of Fire: Judaism, Christianity, and Modernity after the Holocaust." In Auschwitz: Beginning of a New Era?*, edited by Eva Fleischner, KTAV Publishing House, 1977.

28. Brown, Francis, et al. *The Brown-Driver-Briggs Hebrew and English Lexicon*. Hendrickson Publishers, 1994.

29. Harris, R. Laird, et al. *Theological Wordbook of the Old Testament*. Moody Press, 1980.

30. Buttrick, George Arthur, et al., Editors. *The Interpreter's Dictionary of the Bible*. Abingdon Press, 1962.

31. Seow, Choon-Leong. *Job 1-21: Interpretation and Commentary*. Eerdmans, 2013.

32. Keil, Carl Friedrich, and Franz Delitzsch. *Commentary on the Old Testament, Volume IV: Job, Psalms, Proverbs, Ecclesiastes, Song of Songs*. Hendrickson Publishers, 2002.

33. Heiser, Michael S. n.d. *"A Few Thoughts on Job." Dr. Michael S. Heiser*. Accessed December 13, 2024. https://drmsh.com/a-few-

thoughts-on-job/.

34. Pickering, Wes. *"Hold Your Tongue And Cling To Him: An Exegetical Reading of Job 35:1-16"* (master's project, Global Awakening Theological Seminary, 2024).

35. Andersen, Ragnar. *"The Elihu Speeches: Their Place and Sense in the Book of Job."* Tyndale Bulletin 66, no. 1 (2015): 75–94.

36. Ash, Christopher. *Job: The Wisdom of the Cross.* Edited by R. Kent Hughes. Preaching the Word. Wheaton, IL: Crossway, 2014.

37. Clines, David J. A. *Job 1-20. Vol. 17. Word Biblical Commentary.* Nashville, TN: Thomas Nelson, 1989.

38. Hartley, John E. *The Book of Job. The New International Commentary on the Old Testament.* Grand Rapids, MI: William B. Eerdmans, 1988.

39. Piper, John. *"Job: Rebuked in Suffering." Sermons from John Piper (1980–1989).* Minneapolis, MN: Desiring God, 2007.

40. Seow, Choon-Leong. "Elihu's Revelation." *Theology Today* 63, no. 3 (2011): 253–71.

41. Osbeck, Kenneth W. *101 Hymn Stories: The Inspiring True Stories Behind 101 Favorite Hymns.* Kregel Publications, 1982.

42. Spurgeon, Charles Haddon. *Lectures to My Students.* London: Passmore & Alabaster, 1875.

43. Spurgeon, Charles Haddon. *"The Minister's Fainting Fits."* The Sword and the Trowel, 1866.

44. Dallimore, Arnold. *Spurgeon: A New Biography.* Edinburgh: Banner of Truth Trust, 1985.

45. Murray, Iain H. *The Forgotten Spurgeon*. Edinburgh: Banner of Truth Trust, 1973.

46. Athanasius. *On the Incarnation: The Treatise De Incarnatione Verbi Dei*. Translated by a Religious of C.S.M.V., St. Vladimir's Seminary Press, 1977.

47. Grudem, Wayne. *Systematic Theology: An Introduction to Biblical Doctrine*. Zondervan, 1994.

48. Nouwen, Henri J.M.. *The Wounded Healer: Ministry in Contemporary Society*. Image Books, 1979.

49. Brueggemann, Walter. *The Prophetic Imagination*. 2nd ed., Fortress Press, 2001.

50. Wright, N.T. *Jesus and the Victory of God*. Fortress Press, 1996.

51. Holland, Tom. *Dominion: How the Christian Revolution Remade the World*. Basic Books, 2019.

52. Davis, C. Truman. "*The Crucifixion of Jesus: A Medical Perspective*." Arizona Medicine, March, 1965.

53. Stott, John. *The Cross of Christ*. InterVarsity Press, 2006.

54. Edwards, William D., Wesley J. Gabel, and Floyd E. Hosmer. "On the Physical Death of Jesus Christ." *Journal of the American Medical Association*, vol. 255, no. 11, 1986, pp. 1455-1463.

55. Hengel, Martin. *Crucifixion in the Ancient World and the Folly of the Message of the Cross*. Fortress Press, 1977.

56. Metherell, Alexander. *"A Physician Testifies About the Crucifixion."* In Lee Strobel's The Case for Christ. Zondervan, 1998.

57. Nouwen, Henri J. M. *Out of Solitude: Three Meditations on the Christian Life*. Ave Maria Press, 2004, p. 37.

58. Johnson, Sue. *Hold Me Tight: Seven Conversations for a Lifetime of Love*. Little, Brown Spark, 2008.

59. Zimet, Gregory D., et al. "The Multidimensional Scale of Perceived Social Support." *Journal of Traumatic Stress*, 1988.

60. van der Kolk, Bessel. *The Body Keeps the Score: Brain, Mind, and Body in the Healing of Trauma*. Penguin Books, 2014.

61. Cozolino, Louis. *Social Neuroscience and Relationships*. W.W. Norton & Company, 2014.

62. Wright, N.T. *God and the Pandemic: A Christian Reflection on the Coronavirus and Its Aftermath*. Zondervan, 2020.

63. Neimeyer, Robert A. "Meaning Reconstruction in the Wake of Loss: Evolution of a Research Program." *Behavior Modification*, vol. 24, no. 6, 2000, pp. 736–747.

64. Lewis, C.S. *A Grief Observed*. HarperOne, 1961.

65. Kübler-Ross, Elisabeth, and David Kessler. *On Grief and Grieving: Finding the Meaning of Grief Through the Five Stages of Loss*. Scribner, 2005.

66. Boss, Pauline. *The Myth of Closure: Ambiguous Loss in a Time of Pandemic and Change*. W.W. Norton & Company, 2021.

67. Monod, Adolphe. *Jesus Tempted in the Wilderness: Sharing Christ's Victory*. Edited and translated by Constance K. Walker, Solid Ground Christian Books, 2010.

68. Metaxas, Eric. *Bonhoeffer: Pastor, Martyr, Prophet, Spy.* Thomas Nelson, 2010.

69. Bonhoeffer, Dietrich. *Letters and Papers from Prison.* Edited by Eberhard Bethge, SCM Press, 1953.

70. Salisbury, Joyce E. *Perpetua's Passion: The Death and Memory of a Young Roman Woman.* Routledge, 1997.

71. Shewring, W. H. *The Martyrdom of Perpetua and Felicity.* Hassell Street Press, 2021.

72. Murray, Andrew. *Abide in Christ.* Whitaker House, 2003.

73. Lawrence, Brother. *The Practice of the Presence of God.* Whitaker House, 1982.

74. Teresa of Ávila. *The Interior Castle.* Translated by E. Allison Peers, Dover Publications, 2007.

75. Teresa of Ávila. *The Way of Perfection.* Translated by E. Allison Peers, Dover Publications, 2007.

76. Dubay, Thomas. *Fire Within: St. Teresa of Avila, St. John of the Cross, and the Gospel on Prayer.* Ignatius Press, 1989.

77. *Teresa's reflections on spiritual dryness are found in The Book of Her Life,* translated by E. Allison Peers, 3rd ed., Sheed & Ward, 1946.

78. Kavanaugh, Kieran, and Otilio Rodriguez, translators. *The Collected Works of St. Teresa of Avila, Volume One.* ICS Publications, 1987.

79. Williams, Rowan. *Teresa of Avila.* Continuum, 1991.

80. Murray, Andrew. *Abide in Christ.* Fleming H. Revell Company,

1895.

81. *The Holy Bible, English Standard Version.* Crossway, 2001.

82. Ladd, George Eldon. *The Presence of the Future: The Eschatology of Biblical Realism.* Grand Rapids, MI: Eerdmans, 1996.

83. Boyd, Gregory A. *Present Perfect: Finding God in the Now.* Grand Rapids, MI: Zondervan, 2010.

84. Wright, N. T. *Surprised by Hope: Rethinking Heaven, the Resurrection, and the Mission of the Church.* New York: HarperOne, 2008.

85. Moltmann, Jürgen. *Theology of Hope: On the Ground and the Implications of a Christian Eschatology.* Minneapolis, MN: Fortress Press, 1993.

86. Keller, Timothy. *Walking with God Through Pain and Suffering.* New York: Dutton, 2013.

87. Doré, Gustave. *Destruction of Leviathan.* 1865, engraving.

More From The Author

We must overcome a dragon that holds us captive - a dragon called the religious spirit. Journey through "Kill The Dragon" and discover a realm beyond the shackles of religion. Whether you've been wounded by religion or envision a better Church, "Kill The Dragon" offers clarity, healing, and a way forward.

About The Author

Gunter Akridge is an author and pastor with a heart for helping people navigate faith through suffering. Drawing from personal experience, biblical wisdom, and the stories of those who have walked through deep pain, he offers encouragement for anyone struggling to hold onto faith when life falls apart.

www.ingramcontent.com/pod-product-compliance
Lightning Source LLC
Chambersburg PA
CBHW061608120626
46550CB00004B/1655